FOAL
— TO —
FIVE YEARS
Ann Hyland

WARD LOCK

First paperback edition 1992
First published in Great Britain in 1980
by Ward Lock Limited, Villiers House,
41/47 Strand, London WC2N 5JE,
A Cassell Imprint

Reprinted 1982, 1983 (twice), 1985, 1986, 1987,
1989, 1990, 1991, 1993 (twice)

Text filmset in Monophoto Baskerville
by Advanced Filmsetters (Glasgow) Ltd

Printed and bound in Hong Kong by
Everbest Printing Co. Ltd

British Library Cataloguing in Publication Data

Hyland, Ann
  Foal to five years.
  1. Ponies
  I. Title
  636.1′6   SF315

  ISBN 0-7063-7120-8

Frontispiece: A Palomino mare showing the sculpted
ears, large eye and great breadth of forehead denoting
keenness and intelligence inherited from her Arabian
sire. This mare is registered with the Part-bred Arab
Register; her dam was a Thoroughbred/Welsh cross.

Acknowledgments

I should like to thank the following for their help in
various ways whilst I was compiling this book:
Mr John Broughton, MRCVS, BSc, for his help and
guidance on veterinary aspects throughout the book.
Miss Jeanette McKenzie for assistance over showjump-
ing statistics.
The Roughwood House Stud and Gilbert Sturtridge
who own and stand the HIS Premium Stallion 'Piper's
Waite'; Mrs Shuna Mardon of Manar Quarter Horse
Stud; Mr and Mrs N. Harley of the Diablo Quarter
Horse Stud; Mr Bill Frith, Mr Henry Deptford; Miss
Pauline Langford and Summer Solar Fantasy; Mr S.
Humphreys; Mrs J. Thomas; Mrs Jenny Loriston-
Clarke; Mrs Priscilla Leigh; Miss Sally Crossland – all
of whom gave time or facilities for photographing the
horses used in the book.

Ann Hyland

The publishers would like to thank Alison Sherred for
help on the USA sections of the book; and everyone
who supplied photographs.
Black and white photographs by: John Elliott pages 19,
28, 54, 58, 59; Bill and Marylin Galusha page 98; Kit
Houghton page 123; Leslie Lane pages 20, 74, 76–77,
80 and 106; Bob Langrish pages 27, 62, 63, 79, 93 and
105; Jane Miller pages 33, 34, 37, 39, 40, 41, 47, 52 and
57; Equestrian Services Thorney page 80; we would
like to thank Mrs Blake for the use of the Lippen Welsh
Pony Stud, Hampshire, in these photographs; Michael
Port pages 2, 16, 21, 23, 50, 62, 72, 77, 83, 89, 96, 119,
120, 121, 125 and 126; Peter Rossdale pages 9, 10, 11,
32, 38, 42, 62, 110 and 111; Sally-Anne Thompson
pages 14, 15, 16, 21 below, 24, 25, 44–45, 48, 53, 61,
128; John Topham page 65.
Colour photographs by: John Elliott pages 18 below,
86; Kit Houghton pages 18 above, 85; Michael Port
pages 36 below, 104; R. N. Targett page 35; Sally-Anne
Thompson page 36 above, 103, Ann Hyland page 17
below.

Contents

1

Deciding
to breed a foal

Many horse owners, particularly those who have had a beloved animal for a number of years, often think about what they will do in the future when their present horse is ageing and past its peak performance years; more pressingly, when it is well into its teens and no longer able to give the full measure of athletic performance that made it such a wonderful and active companion.

The question of another horse to take Number One's place arises. For many owners the idea of raising a youngster has much appeal, particularly if the current horse still has useful service to offer.

If your present mount is a mare and has given generous and talented service over many years it is only natural that the idea will form of raising a foal from her, thus perpetuating her own line and your own pleasure. The idea will strike many owners at first as a very good move and then later, one fraught with setbacks. Accepting that it can be a very good move, and that the setbacks are far from insurmountable with a know-ledgeable and informed approach, go ahead and explore the possibilities.

First, think out why you want to breed a foal. Is it sentiment, or a real wish to continue a mare's line, enhancing her own qualities by choosing to send her to a good stallion?

As things stand in the horse world today, it is always cheaper to buy in a young horse than to raise one yourself – a very unfair set of circumstances, but an unalterable fact cor-roborated by a study of *Horse and Hound*. However, there are other factors to consider.

There is tremendous satisfaction in being part of the growing up process of the horse you intend as a companion for your leisure time. This is coupled with the pride of knowing that his correct physical, mental, and athletic development is due to you. Much insight into how the mature animal will develop will be gained during the foal and yearling stages, insight which will help you to develop the youngster's good points and prevent less desirable habits forming.

Once you have decided to breed from your mare, there are two major points to consider: the mare herself, her good and her bad points; and what you want from the foal. Will your own riding activities be more, or less, demanding in six years time? Will you want a more, or less, ambitious mount than your mare? Study your mare's conformation. Take a very critical look at it. Assess her good points, and make a careful note of any bad ones that may have affected her physical performance over the years. Having done this, think about how to raise a foal that will be better than its dam. Upgrading is important; your aim should be to send your mare to a stallion that can complement her good and counterbalance less good points.

Going to stud

It is important to realize that when you agree to send a mare to stud you are entering into a contract with the stallion owner, even though a written agreement is not always drawn up. Some studs do send out nomination forms; others accept bookings to their stallions on a verbal basis, while others require a portion of the stud fee as a deposit when the mare is booked in.

The terms under which the stallion stands at stud are printed on his stud card, along with other particulars, such as groom's fee, keep of mares, and usually a clause stating that while the stud will take all reasonable care of the mare no responsibility is accepted for accidents. The contract may be one of the following:

Private Treaty as its name implies, is a matter for individual agreement between the parties concerned.

No Foal Free Return (NFFR) means that if the mare does not conceive during the current season, the stallion owner gives a free return service the following year. This is the most common contract in Britain.

No Foal No Fee means that should the mare not conceive then no stud fee is payable. This form of contract is not usual as there are many factors governing conception, and the cause of infertility more commonly lies with the mare.

The two latter terms are not commonly used in the USA.

Live Foal Guarantee is sometimes offered, often as an additional term to the NFFR. However if this is so, and the mare owner chooses to take this offer, a higher fee is usually asked as there is greater financial risk to the stallion owner.

This is the form of contract used in the USA, and means a foal that stands and nurses. Stud fees are not usually returned. Either the mare may return for service, or occasionally another mare might be substituted.

The above terms of contract often carry the stipulation that if the owner wishes to avail himself of a Free Return under the NFFR or non-payment of stud fee under the NFNF, a certificate of barrenness must be produced by October 1st of the current season.

Return in Season means that the mare can return for further covering during the current season if she fails to settle to service earlier. The 'season' usually runs until October 1st. From the stallion owner's point of view the last named contract is preferable, because it means that the mare's owner is more inclined to do his or her best to get her in foal during the current breeding season, preferably leaving her at the stud for six weeks. Should a mare have to return, naturally a charge will be made for keep.

This contract is used in the USA. It can cost one-and-a-half times the amount of a *Live Foal Guarantee*, but may not carry a pregnancy guarantee.

Since the outbreak of Contagious Equine Metritis in Britain in 1977, many British studs require the mare to be swabbed beforehand to make sure she is free of any venereal disease. Obtain your veterinary surgeon's advice once you know the requirements of the stud to which you are sending your mare.

In the USA most reputable breeding farms will require a health certificate, a negative Coggins test and a negative uterine culture.

Stud facilities and stallion management
You will also want to know how the stud is managed, and how the actual covering is handled. If you choose to have your mare kept at grass whilst she is at stud, do notice, when you go to see the stallion, whether the fields are well fenced. How many mares run on how much acreage? Do mares with foals at foot run with barren and maiden mares? This could cause jealousy problems. What is the state of the pasture? If it is good, and there are not too many mares in each field there is less likelihood of it being worm-infested. If it is overgrazed and overstocked it is probably very wormy.

Ask how the stallion is managed. Does he run with his mares? Or are all his coverings done in hand, which means both mare and stallion are under control during the service.

It is worth asking what a particular stallion's fertility rating is. The horse is not the most fertile animal, particularly when man arranges his matings. It is well known that the stallion who runs out with his mares has a higher fertility rate than the stallion who covers in hand. The stallion running out is closer to nature and instinctively knows the right time for each mare. In the case of the stallion covering in hand it is not that the

Before a mare is mated by the stallion she is introduced across a teasing board.

stallion's fertility is any lower when he is covering in hand, but it is not always possible for man to pinpoint the exact time when mating should occur with the highest chance of the mare conceiving. Knowledgeable management is a must when the stud does not run its stallion out, which is not normal with large breeds, or very valuable stallions, as there is too much risk of accident.

Acquaint yourself with all the particulars relating to the stud to which you are sending your mare well in advance of her arrival, and let the stud owners know when that will be.

The mare's sexual cycle

Now you must decide the approximate time when you want the foal born. This will depend on three things: the mare's sexual cycle; the amenities you have; and the economics. Spring is the usual time for foals to be born, when the grass is greening and rich, and the sun warm; feeding will also be cheaper. However, you may want the foal born earlier in the year. This means more feeding, and more work, in that mare and foal will need to be kept stabled till the weather improves. If the mare is your only riding horse it has the advantage that the foal can be weaned in time to leave much of the summer and all autumn to enjoy riding her. The choice is yours.

It is always helpful to be able to tell the stud groom the length of the mare's sexual

Mares in heat accept the attentions of the male, raising the tail and 'squatting' on his approach.

cycle. The average complete cycle is approximately twenty-one to twenty-three days, with a mare being in season from five to seven days, and out for sixteen days. However, there are many mares who can come either side of the average, with shorter or longer cycles.

Cycles vary according to the time of the year, being erratic or non-existent in the cold winter months. They become obvious as the days lengthen, with the in-season days being very marked in late spring and early summer, which is the natural time, in the wild, for mares to be covered and to hold to service. Lengthening days and strengthening sun influence the natural cycle of mares, which is why in Thoroughbred, and some showing studs, electric warmth and light are used in the mares' stabling in winter and spring. The best time for covering is the penultimate, or the last day of the cycle, which is when the egg ruptures, and unites with the sperm. The rupturing of the egg makes the mare go 'out of season'.

It is therefore important to know the approximate length of the mare's cycle. Most stallions have many mares to cover; at the height of the breeding season they may have to cope with several mares a day, so planning mare load is important. Spermatozoa have a limited life which is not necessarily the same for each stallion, nor always the same for a particular stallion. The average life is around forty-eight hours. Therefore the mare who is covered only once during her cycle is very lucky indeed if she holds to that service, unless such service is at exactly the right moment of her sexual cycle.

If you intend leaving the mare at stud for the full six-week period after service, at which time she can be tested and found to be either in foal or empty, you can leave everything to the stud. If, however, you intend only leaving the mare whilst she is in season and then taking her home it is up to you to arrange when to return her for 'trying'. It is not enough to have her 'tried' once only, at three weeks. Her cycle could be shorter or longer than the 'book average'. Several trying sessions will be needed at intervals of two or three days, so it is better to leave her at the stud for long enough to make sure that she has held, or turned to service, when she can be served again. This is probably the one foal in a lifetime from your riding mare so you want to help the mare hold to service. It can be helpful to ask the vet to give her an internal examination before sending her to stud, to make sure all is well. To help her conceive a luteinizing hormone may be used. Six weeks after the service an internal pregnancy examination may be done; there is no conclusive evidence that this will cause the

Mating.

mare to abort – if she does so it will probably be for another reason.

If your mare appears to have held to service you should still keep a watch for signs of imminent oestrus for several months as occasionally a mare will slip her foal, or even absorb it. If this is detected early enough in the breeding season there will be time to return her to the stud. If this has happened, to help her hold to the next service you could ask the vet to give her progesterone once she is found to be in foal again. This can be a short-term injection or long-term implant. Occasionally an in-foal mare will come into season, but when presented to the stallion she will not stand for service.

Preparing the mare for service
The mare should go to stud in good condition. She should have been recently wormed. Her shoes should be removed and her hind feet trimmed smooth to prevent any lacerations to the stallion should she kick during service; most mares will not kick if they are receptive, but maiden mares may do at first, through fear. If your mare is a known kicker, you are duty bound to warn the stud manager; also if she is very bossy at pasture. She should be easy to catch. Valuable time can be wasted trying to catch a mare before service, and the stud fee is for the service only, not for teaching your mare manners! She should also load easily into a trailer or horse box. Although it is not mandatory for some-one from the stud to help you load your mare when she leaves, it is a gesture nearly always made. It is incredible how many mares will not load. Stud staff waste hours giving a hand with these ill-mannered animals; so do teach your mare to load before you send her to stud. She will be welcomed back there, rather than her return dreaded!

A mare going to stud should be fit but not fat. Being overweight is often a cause of infertility. When she returns from stud, worm her, even if she is not due for worming.

2
Choosing a stallion

The first quality to look for in a stallion is soundness; it is foolish to send your good riding mare to a stallion who has not proved himself capable of standing up to hard work. Show ring wins are fine, but only if performance under saddle follows can a stallion be said to have proved himself and be suitable to sire sound working offspring.

Assuming that your mare has basically good conformation and is sound, consider next what type and breed of stallion to choose.

First: the Thoroughbred; the Arabian; the Quarterhorse; and the Anglo-Arab, comments on each applying equally to mares and stallions. It is usually advisable to send a purebred mare to a stallion of the same breed, but a straight cross can be good, particularly with the Thoroughbred. Unless you specifically want to produce a racehorse or a hunter-chaser or a point-to-point horse, it is better to breed an outcross; to produce an animal with the good qualities of the Thoroughbred and the chosen stallion. Be clear about what you want in the foal. See as many stallions as possible. Ask to see the progeny of each stallion and enquire about his performance and that of his offspring.

A Thoroughbred stallion with good bone and substance.

This will give you an idea of what you are likely to breed especially if you see some of the mares.

It used to be a legal requirement for a stallion standing at stud to be licensed, by the Ministry of Agriculture Fisheries and Food, as being free from hereditary defects and of suitable conformation. This is no longer the case. Any prospective breeder is, however, advised to check that the stallion of choice has been inspected by a qualified veterinary surgeon according to the criteria laid down by the respective breed society. If this inspection is satisfactory the breed society will issue a stallion certificate and resulting progeny will be entitled to registration in the pure or part bred section of the named breed. If the stallion fails the veterinary inspection, the progeny will not be accepted for future registry.

Do not be satisfied with a verbal assurance but ask to see the stallion's breed society certificate.

A Welsh Cob (Section D) stallion. A cob stallion of this type makes an excellent cross on to a Thoroughbred mare to produce a riding horse of great activity, good temperament and considerable hardiness. Formerly used for trotting races, the Welsh cob has a free, active trot and is now very successful in competitive driving, combining courage with intelligence and an equable temperament.

The stallion

The Thoroughbred

Ideally, look for a Thoroughbred stallion of 15.2 to 16.1 hands, and with a bodyweight of between 499 and 544 kg (1100 and 1200 lb). In the USA stallions of 16 hands plus may be preferred; the tendency is to breed larger horses. He should have good bone and good hooves, be relatively short in the back and deep through the barrel, girth and chest giving plenty of room for heart and lungs. His hindquarters should be muscular and in proportion to the rest of him – not all forehand and fading away behind. His neck should be lightly crested and the head should meet the neck at an angle that permits good wind passage. The head should be refined; the eye large and generous; muzzle neat; and the jawline of good depth. Pay particular attention to hooves, as Thoroughbreds are inclined to have shallow feet with flat soles and a thin wall; the horn is sometimes shelly and prone to splitting and flaking. Be very particular about temperament. Although some Thoroughbreds have beautiful temperaments and kind dispositions, others can be nervous, flighty and irascible. Remember that Thoroughbreds generally require above-average feeding and grazing.

The Arabian

There are three distinct types of Arabian. Many are of the very rounded heavily fleshed type with somewhat coarser limbs; others are racy and lean, with too much daylight underneath them, giving the impression of being rather insubstantial. The best combines both types; a type which is streamlined, has very good bone, but is very refined. Arabians range from 14 hands up to the rare 16 hand animal. The current trend in breeding is to produce a horse of about 15 hands plus. With greater size it sometimes happens that some

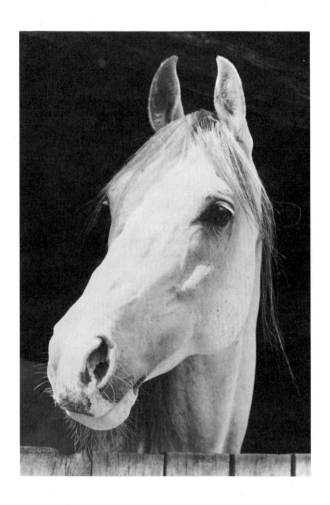

Purebred Arabian stallion, American-bred, with a highly intelligent head and large kind eye, showing a friendly and alert disposition. The inward-tipping ears are characteristic of the breed. This horse is a long distance champion.

type and quality are lost. The stallion to look for is one that has size, but still maintains quality without any hint of coarseness, or lack of substance. A good guide is weight in relation to height. A 15 hand Arabian weighing around 408 kg (900 lb) will be substantial enough without being either coarse or flimsy.

When crossed with native ponies or non-Arab mares of their own size, many Arabian stallions have the bonus of adding considerable size to their offspring, so do not reject an Arabian because he is small.

Above: The Appaloosa stallion 'Rodega Tobias' in action. This is a popular breed in the USA and increasingly so in Britain, this striking looking horse was developed by Indians in the Palouse Valley in Orgeon. It is a good all-rounder, noted for its hardiness and stamina; the introduction of some Arab blood has made it a first-class riding horse.

Below: A pure bred quarterhorse gelding, 'Chunky's Sovereign', in the peak of condition. This is the most popular breed in the USA, is exported to Australia, and is gaining recognition in Britain. Its docile, easy-going disposition, toughness, and muscular strength combined with refinement make it good for cross-breeding, particularly with a lighter horse.

Above: An Irish Draught mare ready to be shown in-hand at the Dublin Horse Show. For centuries this breed has been the basis of the magnificent hunters and all-purpose riding horses produced in Ireland. Many of today's international showjumpers have been bred in Ireland and are half or quarter-bred Irish Draught.

Right: Showing a mare and foal in-hand. Young stock should be used to being handled, and accustomed to the environment of the show ground, before being taken into the ring.

Real bonuses with the Arabian are the superb temperament he hands down and the extravagant gaits of which he is capable, coupled with the important attributes of toughness and the ability to endure great stress, while the Arabs' intelligence is renowned. My own experience has been that Arabian, and Part-Arabian, youngstock do learn more quickly than other breeds, although they are sometimes over-eager to go on to the next lesson, becoming bored with too much repetition and wanting to go to an advancement they are not ready for. If you can cope with and enjoy this attribute then the Arabian is for you.

'You can take a white horse anywhere'—a well-known purebred Arab stallion.

The Hunters' Improvement Society stallion

Under the system operated by the Hunters' Improvement Society, each stallion must pass a stringent conformation and soundness test before he is approved and allocated to a specific district where he will stand for the season. If you wish to use a Thoroughbred, always look into the possibilities of getting a nomination to your local HIS stallion. Many Thoroughbreds who have raced have acquired various unsoundnesses, curbs, bowed tendons, etc., that have caused them to break down in training. Early speed being a requirement in the racing industry, the breakdown may have been because of being worked too early or because the horse was basically deficient in conformation. Avoid any stallion that has broken down due to a

Above: A good example of a Hunters' Improvement Society Premium stallion. In Britain the HIS scheme makes available high quality Thoroughbred stallions at reduced fees, thus encouraging private horse owners to produce good quality young stock.

Above right: An Anglo-Arab stallion produced here for the show ring. His off-fore pastern clearly shows ermine marking. This superb stallion has passed on his substance and quality to foals out of many different types of mare (*see* photo page 36).

conformation weakness which could be passed on to his progeny. Blemishes caused by accidents are different, and should not deter anyone from using an otherwise excellent stallion.

The Appaloosa

The Appaloosa is a breed that is becoming increasingly popular in Great Britain. Noted for its variegated coat, striped hooves, mottled skin around the eyes, muzzle and genitalia and for the white sclera around the eye, the true Appaloosa is a recognised breed and must not be confused with just any spotted horse. The British Appaloosa Society has done sterling work with breed improvement and, as with the Quarterhorse, there are distinct types available, the two most notable being the hunter type and the western type. An Appaloosa crossed with a Thoroughbred or Quarterhorse will, produce a horse with excellent athletic ability. The Appaloosa's colour genes are a strong line of inheritance and even if a solid colour results in the first generation the subsequent generation is more likely to exhibit the characteristic spotted colouration. It would be advisable to study the

Appaloosa colour patterns and genetics before deciding on a stallion of a particular coat pattern.

The Quarterhorse

Horses of this breed, like the Arabian, also fall into three distinct types. There is the short, stocky, very heavily muscled type ranging in height from 14.2 to 15 hands and weighing well over 450 kg (1,000 lb). The second type of Quarterhorse will be upwards of 15 hands, still heavily muscled, though not as stocky as the former and show somewhat more refinement and be in the range of 450 kg (1,000 lb) to 590 kg (1,200 lb). This is the type most often seen in US Quarterhorse events and is increasingly seen in British events. The third type will be very breedy, usually with a heavy infusion of Thoroughbred blood in his recent pedigree. He may weigh no more than the middle type but could reach 16 hands plus, as the current trend is to breed for height, particularly as in America the Quarterhorse is showing great aptitude for jumping and eventing. There are representatives of all three types in Britain.

Quarterhorses have classically good dispositions and are tractable and docile. They are good doers, costing considerably less to keep than most breeds of similar size. Short distance speed is one of their characteristics as well as tremendous power in the hindquarters, often massively muscular.

The Quarterhorse makes a good cross for a rather light-boned mare, but is not as good for one somewhat gross, or top heavy. Faults of the breed are that some Quarterhorses do not have sufficient bone below the knee, and some hooves tend to be rather too small and boxy for the weight of the body. Certain types lack the really good stride needed in many equestrian events today, yet others, especially the type with Thoroughbred blood, have great scope. If you can use a scopey Quarterhorse stallion, with the breed's superb disposition, a real winner could result from the cross.

As with any breed the qualities of soundness and tractability of temperament are vital.

The Anglo-Arab

As its name implies this is a breed containing only Thoroughbred and Arabian blood – it combines the size and speed of the Thoroughbred with the greater intelligence and more equable temperament of the Arabian, has excellent bone, good conformation and sound, hard feet. In a good specimen of the breed these qualities will be present. In choosing an Anglo-Arab stallion, pay great attention to temperament, as though they may be superb, some can be very excitable, combining the volatility of the Thoroughbred with the high spirits of the Arabian. The stallion's temperament may be passed on to his offspring, even if the dam's is equable.

The mare

The hunter

A high percentage of 'family horses' come under this heading. A hunter mare is likely to be either a half or three-quarter Thoroughbred. She will stand between 15.1 and 16.1 hands, have a fair amount of substance, and carry enough flesh to be rounded but not gross. The higher proportion of 'hot blood' she has, the less coarse her bone and the more refined her lines. The half-bred mare will probably have a more docile temperament than the three-quarter-bred. If the mare is 'cobby' she could tend to be overweight and her gait could be stilted. Usually the less proportion of 'hot blood', the less elegant her stride, and improvement should be sought in the foal.

The Part-Arab

For many decades Arabian blood has been used to infuse quality and is now present in just about all types of crossbreeds. Good riding horses of Part-Arab ancestry proliferate, with many of the crosses being achieved by using an Arabian stallion on a Thoroughbred cross native mare, or on a coarser type of mare to give quality. A native pony mare crossed with an Arabian produces an animal of considerable size, substance and quality.

Above right: A New Forest-cross-Arab mare. The Arab blood has increased her height to 15 hands (her dam was 13 hands). She shows considerable refinement and substance but kept some of the best pony qualities of short cannons and good bone. A good breeding prospect, she produced a top-quality foal by a Quarterhorse stallion.

Below right: A half-Quarterhorse mare. She shows the quiet and kind Quarterhorse temperament and very developed quarters. This mare is wearing a bosal which controls the horse with light pressure over the nose and under the chin, with minimal pressure at the sides when the reins are used.

Above: A New Forest pony mare with a nice kind eye; like the Fell pony, this breed can be put to a Thoroughbred or Arab stallion, or, to produce a pony foal, to a pony stallion. To produce a larger animal, a quality stallion with a compact body, strong in shoulder, quarters and length of neck should be used to enhance this mare's qualities.

Above right: A Welsh Mountain Pony (Section A) mare. This is the prettiest of the native breeds, noted for soundness and stamina, and is good for cross-breeding with a larger stallion.

Below right: A Fell pony mare. As with all the larger British native pony breeds the Fell pony can be bred up or down, to produce either a pony or a horse, according to the stallion used.

For a Part-bred Arab mare, great care should be taken in choosing the right stallion if you are not to end up with a hotch-potch. The infusion of Arabian blood will already have given a certain elegance of line and gait, but it will also have given a lively temperament, so the temperament of the stallion is very important.

The native pony

The native pony or crossbred native pony of the larger breeds is most frequently found as the family riding pony, in particular the New Forest which can go up to 14.2 hands, and the Connemara of similar height. The largest of the Welsh ponies, the Welsh cob, the Highland, and the Fell and Dale also come into this category. Native ponies have considerable substance, are longlived, hardy and usually tractable. They may carry excessive flesh, so laminitis can result. Their movement may reflect too much 'pony gait'; this is important when considering a stallion.

Choose one with a good long elastic stride. Many ponies although tractable, also have a way of not giving their best if their owners accept less than their best, and they are usually crafty enough to realize the owner is fooled. Look for the most generous nature possible in the stallion allied with a certain *élan*. As an example, the Welsh Cob/Thoroughbred cross is proving particularly good.

In the USA, other popular breeds of stallion are the Morgan, Saddlebred, Appaloosa and Tennessee Walker.

Making the choice

It is now up to you as the mare owner to make the final choice of which stallion to use. Give much thought to what may result of the mating. Betterment is the aim. If your vet is a knowledgeable horse veterinarian, he should give sound advice as to what points to look for in the stallion and what to avoid.

The overriding qualities needed in any horse are: basic good conformation, good disposition, and good temperament (a horse can have the former and still be flighty) allied with soundness. Do not use a stallion lacking in any of these. You will need to consider:

(1) The size you want the foal to grow to.

(2) The physical attributes. Do you want a light, medium, or heavier type of horse?

(3) The economics of feeding. Generally, the more highly-bred the horse, the more feed it will need; the more native, relatively, the less. Some breeds have a higher metabolic rate than others.

(4) The length of stride required. Here it pays to see a horse running free, if possible. Many horses, badly schooled and ridden, never exhibit their true stride length.

(5) How you intend to use your youngster. Be sure to choose a stallion which can compensate for any weaknesses of conformation your mare may have.

A stallion with progeny that have proved themselves under saddle is always preferable to one that may be better looking but has done less, or produced nothing to distinguish himself. A stallion is best judged by his offspring's capabilities.

Do not believe that to be fit, a stallion must also be fat. This is not good. It proves nothing other than that the stallion eats well, and could be an indication that he is unfit and never worked hard. If so why? Any covering stallion benefits from being ridden, or exercised sufficiently to tone his muscles up and give his lungs, heart and limbs the chance to work.

Another point is that some mare owners think a stallion should exhibit a pugnacious attitude and appear full of very wasteful energy. Underworked, overfed and under-disciplined stallions may exhibit these traits. They are not impressive. Always choose a stallion that has worked, is fit physically, and mentally relaxed, so that his true easy-going temperament is apparent, even if this does not match the old-fashioned idea of stallion behaviour. You will get a much better idea of how your youngster will behave if, knowing your own mare, you can also see the real temperament of her foal's sire.

Buying a foal

Not everyone who enters into such a project has the mare to breed from. For those who wish to raise a foal to maturity the job starts with a weanling foal they have purchased.

The early chapters of this book will offer a good guide as to what to look for in the foal you wish to buy. Make up your mind as to the breed, type within a breed, size in height and also in weight, disposition and temperament that you wish to have in the foal you intend purchasing. Give careful consideration to buying the type best suited for the major

Warmblood mare and foal. If this mare were put to a Purebred Arab or Thoroughbred stallion you would inject considerable additional quality.

work you intend doing when the foal has grown up. A study of its parents and siblings will be helpful here. It is no good falling for a sweet little foal with an engaging personality and then finding that you allowed your judgment to be clouded and the foal grows up into an adult horse inadequate for the requirements of your chosen equestrian field.

Having made up your mind about the type of foal you want, start investigating the possibility of purchasing a suitable youngster. There are several channels open to prospect-ive purchasers. Scan through the pages of the horse magazines, but do remember that advertisements are often very cleverly and attractively worded. If you are living in a rural or semi-rural area the local weekly newspaper often has more to offer and within a reasonable distance from home, than the weekly national paper. The same local weekly newspaper will also carry semi-display advertisements of various studs that you could make arrangements to visit to view prospective animals. If you intend purchasing a foal that is a pure or a part-bred of any specific breed it is worthwhile writing to the breed association involved to get a list of studs that have horses for sale. There is a list of these at the back of this book. The breed association contacted will only give you a list, not a recommendation as to who to purchase from, as the secretary must be impartial in

A foal a few weeks old showing how the body has begun to fill out and the legs, now practically as long as the mare's, to strengthen.

help given. However a little homework amongst horsey friends will supply added information. If you are already well into a group of people whose main interest is horses there will be plenty of other opportunities of hearing of who has what for sale.

Having given a few likely sources for finding a foal for sale it is essential that great care should be taken in making the actual choice and that advice be sought from a competent authority. Your vet should be asked for his advice and when the time comes to close the deal he should be approached for his professional opinion. A little money spent now could save a lot of expense and heartache later. Your vet may also have a list of foals for sale and know who to approach

and if he is also aware of your needs and capabilities he may be able to suggest a good choice of future mount for you.

If you have a good friend whose judgment you respect take him or her along when you go 'foal shopping'. Alternatively be prepared to pay a professional horseman a fee for his advice and time spent on a search for a foal. Remember the stud owner wants to sell the foal so the good points will be stressed and the less good ones toned down. However a reputable stud should have its clients' good at heart because a satisfied purchaser is a good form of advertising for the stud in the future. At a good stud the quality of the foal will more than likely be reflected in the price with the better foals commanding a higher price. It is quite common when buying from a stud that fillies will be more expensive than colts, unless a particular colt is good enough to be kept entire. When buying from a private party the price of a filly will not be appreciably more than that of a colt.

The price range for a foal is vast. The best animal does not necessarily cost the most, and frequently the less than best fetch too high a price. Do bear in mind though that a breeder has the right to expect a fair return for the product he or she is selling. The price you pay should cover the keep for a mare for eighteen months, the stud fee for the stallion who covered her, the veterinary costs involved for an in-foal mare and for the foal itself, and any charges on top of the stud fee. There should also be a fair margin of profit for the breeder. It appals me that buyers feel they should be able to purchase a foal for less than the feed cost for a mare for a year. Breeders are not in the very costly business of breeding only to make a gift of their mare's offspring. A word of advice; a cheap foal may work out to be very expensive in the long run as a low price is not always a bargain price. It may be a weedy animal, have poor conformation, or even a poor health history.

One way in which the purchaser of a foal scores over a breeder is that he or she can actually see what is on offer rather than hoping the much loved mare put to the best available stallion will produce a superb offspring. In looking for the superb foal great attention must be paid to the dam and to the sire. In purchasing you will be able to look for a mare that is as close to ideal conformation and with as good a temperament and disposition as possible. It will not be necessary to complement her shortcomings by counterbalancing these with strong points in the stallion. However do bear in mind that the stud owner may have done just that when sending her to the stallion of his choice. You will have the facility of choosing if you think the mare is the right type, and if not you can continue your search. Where the stallion is not resident at the stud it is a good idea to see if you can visit the stud where he stands. Also enquire, and if possible see, about other of his offspring particularly from mares similar to the animal which is the dam of the foal you are thinking of buying.

Do not settle on the first foal you see, but alternatively do not see so many that you become bewildered about what you really want. Word will get around if you waste too many people's time viewing foal after foal.

When buying the foal enquire about his veterinary and handling history. When was he last wormed and with which product? Are his anti-tetanus shots up to date? Has he been vaccinated against equine influenza? Has he had his feet trimmed and how is he with a farrier? Does he stand tied up? Has he any naughty habits that need watching? At weaning time it would be rather unusual if he was a little paragon; and a naughty trick, as opposed to downright bad temper and lack of civility, can be corrected by firmness. A foal well-handled from birth will be easier to train.

3
Caring for the in-foal mare

When your mare returns home from the stud treat her exactly as before. The fact that she is now carrying a foal does not mean she has to go into retirement for the whole of her pregnancy and while she is lactating.

If you normally turn her out with other horses, including geldings, continue to do so. There is no conclusive evidence that running an in-foal mare with a gelding will cause her to abort. Moreover, should the mare abort for any reason, the fact of her running out with a gelding could be a bonus, because if she comes into season she will almost certainly 'show' to him, thus letting you know in good time to send her back to the stallion.

If your mare is used to a very active life and is ridden hard, it is quite in order to expect her to resume her normal work load until about half way through her pregnancy. This includes jumping, long distance riding (*endurance* riding is not open to pregnant mares), hunting (cubbing and the early part of the season only). However, if your mare is normally used to light work only, it is better to keep to her normal routine.

At about half-way through pregnancy, strenuous work should gradually diminish, though normal hacking can be continued. Up till about a month before foaling, she can still do light work, just to keep her muscles in trim. Once all work ceases, she must have plenty of time to exercise herself. Even though very few horses do truly exercise themselves, the freedom of a field or paddock helps to keep muscles toned.

Feeding the in-foal mare

In early pregnancy feed the mare her normal rations. During the first two-thirds of pregnancy the foetus only attains approximately one-third of its final size. In the final third of her term, when the work load has greatly decreased, the rations should not be drasti-

cally cut back. Naturally, if the mare was previously working very hard she would have been getting a grain ration commensurate with her physical output, and at the tailing off of work her grain ration can be cut down. During the last third of pregnancy, however, when the foetus is growing rapidly, the mare will need a boost in feeding levels, especially as by now grazing will be poor. As she will have been your riding horse during the summer, she will not, or should not, have put on excessive weight which is nature's way of preparing an animal for the winter months. When man interferes with nature he has to balance any deficit by extra feeding. Different heights, breeds, and types of horse and pony need feeding differently; but a very good guide for the average horse of about 15 to 15.2 hands weighing about 408 kg (900 lb) to 454 kg (1,000 lb) would be as follows:

Rations are shown as per 45 kg (100 lb) of body weight

WORK	GRAIN	HAY
maintenance or light work up to one hour a day	0.23 kg (0.50 lb)	0.68 kg (1.50 lb)
two hours average work	0.36 kg (0.80 lb)	0.68 kg (1.50 lb)
three to four hours average or two hours hard work	0.45 kg (1.00 lb)	0.68 kg (1.50 lb)
medium hard work up to six hours steady or three hours hard work	0.56 kg (1.25 lb)	0.56 kg (1.25 lb)
work under stress such as jumping, hunting, long distance riding	0.68 kg (1.50 lb)	0.56 kg (1.25 lb)

This is only a rough guide, as every animal is an individual and should be treated as such. Some are particularly 'good doers', others fussy feeders; nor does it take into account any percentage of keep gained from grazing.

Using this scale, feed normally for the first half of pregnancy, step the feed up to the next bracket for the next quarter and during the

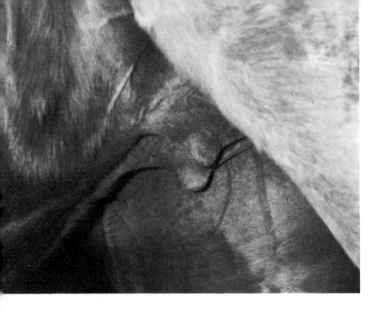

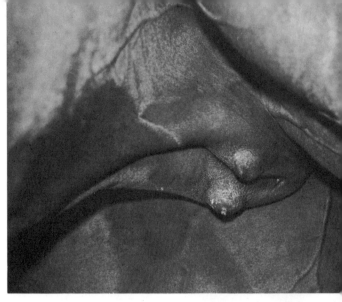

The udder starts to increase in size about five weeks before foaling.

'Wax' may be seen on the end of the teat when foaling is imminent.

last stages treat the mare as if she is in medium to hard work at 0.56 kg (1.25 lb) grain per 45 kg (100 lb) of her normal body weight. If you feel she needs any additives in the form of extra minerals or vitamins get your veterinary surgeon's advice. Roughly one month before foaling give the mare an anti-tetanus booster, which will provide the foal with approximately three months immunity.

The length of equine pregnancy is approximately eleven months, usually a little over. However, some mares can foal earlier than eleven months, and a ten-month foal need cause no worry. Some go up to and over a year; there is no cause for concern if the mare seems bright and comfortable.

Signs of approaching parturition

A sign of approaching birth is that several weeks before, the mare's rib cage will appear to become suddenly distended and the outline of her ribs may be apparent. Also, the stomach-bulge will seem to shift to a lower position and be very prominent towards the flanks. At this time the foal's movements can

Right: The foal is born with a soft horn forming finger-like projections from the sole. These soon disappear once the foal is on its feet. They protect the uterus from injury during foetal life.

often be seen. A fortnight to a week before the actual birth, the mare's udder will start to enlarge. Some mares start to 'bag up' as much as a month before foaling. A few days after the beginning of udder enlargement there will be minute particles of a clear substance on the teats. This is not to be confused with the 'waxing up', which is of an opaque substance and occurs any time from forty-eight to four hours before birth.

Around two weeks before foaling time, the mare's hindquarters will show a marked weight loss, and about four days before birth, the change will become even more marked, with muscles at the root of the tail and over the hindquarters falling away so that the mare looks very 'poor'. This is the outward sign that inwardly the mare is preparing for foaling, by the relaxing of her muscles.

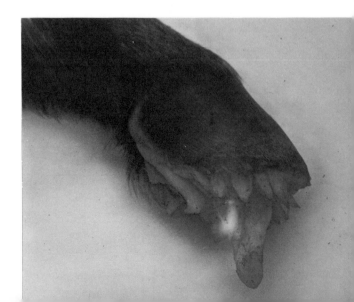

During the last few days the vulva will relax.

If she is still out with other horses when these marked signs of approaching birth are evident, separate her from them. Although text books give time spans for these impending signs, nature can, and often does, hurry things up. Should a mare unexpectedly foal in a field with others, there is great danger of the others' curiosity sparking off quarrels amongst themselves, trying to get to the newborn foal, possibly causing a fatal accident. Remember, domestic horses are kept under unnatural and confined conditions, whereas native pony mares, running wild, can go off to a secluded spot to foal.

There are two schools of thought as to whether a mare should foal in or out. If your pasture is absolutely safe – is clean, has no

Slight anxiety and pawing the ground are signs of impending parturition. Native ponies such as this Welsh pony mare are sometimes better left to foal outside if the weather is dry and the ground clean. This mare is foaling quite early in the year and still has her shaggy winter coat.

wire, no ditches, no fences under which a newborn foal could roll, and if the weather is really clement and the mare happy to be out, there is less chance of an infection setting up. However, unless you propose camping out, it is difficult to check on the mare. If the mare foals in, she should do so in the box she is used to, or moved to well before foaling, so that she will be at ease in it. No box which houses horses can be sterile, but naturally it should be as clean as possible with plenty of bedding, and draught free. If you normally

Normal presentation. The forefeet appear first and then the muzzle.

The birth

use shavings or sawdust for bedding, switch to straw as a precaution against the newborn foal's nostrils getting clogged with fine dust or particles of bedding. If you have very deep litter on the floor, you can top it with a generous layer of straw. As the birth approaches, remove all hay nets, buckets, etc. Any hay can be fed off the floor.

When foaling is imminent, check on the mare frequently, but do not keep disturbing her, especially if she is of a nervous disposition. For your own peace of mind inform your vet that the foal is on its way. He will then know in advance that you will call him out if needed, and if he goes out on another call, will leave a telephone number where he can be contacted. Keep a second telephone

34

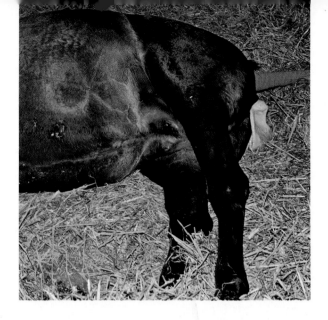

It is best to have a mare foal in a properly prepared foaling box unless she is a native breed or a hardy cross-bred.

Above: After the restlessness of early labour the mare lies down on her side. The two front hooves are beginning to emerge in a 'diving' position, covered by the membrane.

Above right: Most of the foal has emerged and it has broken free of the membrane. If, when the foal's head and shoulders are well clear, it has not broken free of the membrane by itself, an attendant may break it around the nose. *The membrane should not be cleared before this stage*, in case the foal slips back inside the mare.

Right: Welcomed and nuzzled encouragingly by its mother, the foal will soon make its first attempt to rise.

Below: The contented mare acknowledges her wet, newborn foal. Usually she will lick it dry, thus also encouraging its circulation; if not, it will need drying with a towel.

Above: A Thoroughbred mare with her day-old foal in one of a series of special paddocks at a stud in Kentucky, USA. With the special care given to Thoroughbred stock, foals develop especially quickly. This type of fencing is the safest as the bottom bar is low enough for the foal to be unable to roll under it.

Right: A nice quality Hanoverian mare with her well-grown son by an Anglo-Arab stallion (see photograph page 21), who has passed on his quality and refinement to add to the strength and substance of the Hanoverian dam.

number – that of his colleague or another practice – that you can call in case of his being away on another emergency. Just before foaling the mare will get very restless, keep on lying down and getting up again, breaking out into a sweat, and finally lying down for the actual birth. Once this has started she may even get up again and then go down once more. The first signs will be that the waters will break. This will shortly be followed by the caul through which you

Once the shoulders are through the foal slips out comparatively easily, partially covered in membrane. It will struggle free and break the umbilical cord or this may be done by the mare's movement.

should be able to see the front hooves, which will pierce the membrane. The nose then appears, followed very quickly by forelegs, head and shoulders. After the shoulders, the rest of the birth happens very quickly indeed. The whole thing, provided there are no setbacks, will take from fifteen to thirty minutes. If the mare strains to no avail do not try dealing with the situation yourself, but get your vet out immediately. Home therapy during foaling is best left to those who have

Below: A mare becoming acquainted with her foal soon after foaling.

Right: Starting to suck. A foal will take anything from fifteen to ninety minutes to have its first drink.

experience, otherwise unnecessary damage could result.

When the foal is free of the mare, it will still be attached to her by the umbilical cord. *Do not cut this.* It is most important that blood from the placenta runs back to the foal. It will rupture of its own accord when the foal gets to its feet.

The afterbirth should also come away cleanly within a couple of hours. Many mares cleanse well before that. If the mare seems in danger of stepping on the afterbirth while it is still attached to her, tie it up at about hock level so that it will come away naturally. If she has not cleansed within ten hours after foaling she will need veterinary attention.

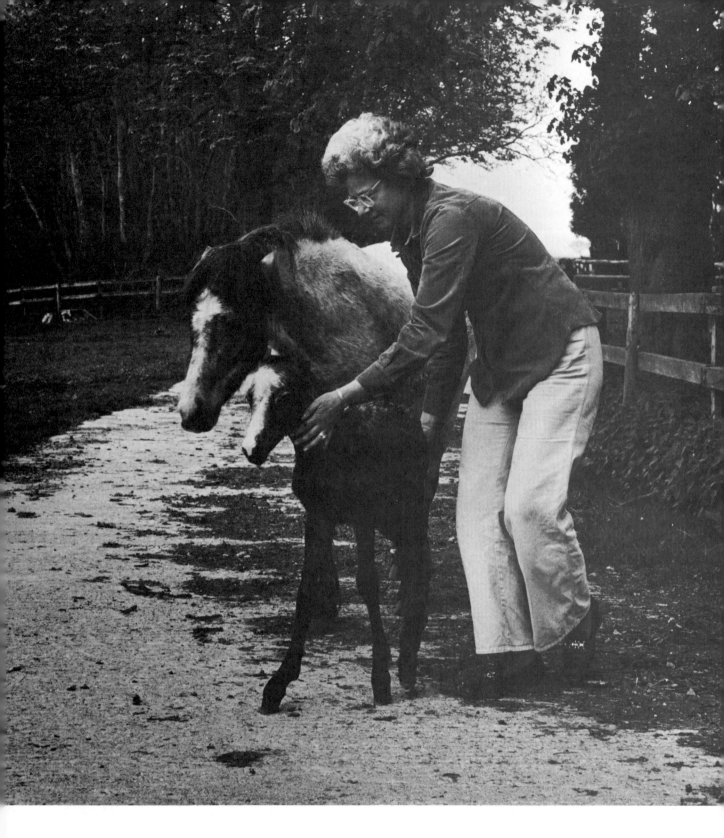

Once the afterbirth is expelled remove it, together with any soiled bedding. Examine it carefully for completeness and abnormalities, if in doubt keep it to show to the vet, then either bury it or burn it. The mare will attend to the foal herself so there should be no need to dry him off with towels, particularly if everything is normal and bedding is ample.

The commonest time for foaling is in the early daylight hours, but if you are lucky enough to be present at the birth (though it is

likely that the mare will surprise you between check-over visits), stay long enough to see that the foal is on its feet and sucking. If it has much difficulty in gaining its feet, you can help by cradling it around chest and quarters. You can also help guide it to the

Left: Asking mother to move her foal on to softer ground.

Above: The mare licks the foal to dry it off.

41

A twin foal, for which the mare has not enough milk, is fed by means of a bottle and artificial teat.

mare's udder. Foals always seem to know the general direction, but that last bit of finding mum's milk takes some doing. It would have been helpful if during the 'bagging up' process you had handled the udder and a few days before expected foaling, placed warm cloths on it. This will accustom the mare to being felt in that region and make her less worried by the foal's attentions. If your mare is a maiden it is quite possible that she may refuse to let the foal suckle at first, squealing and moving away every time it tries. If this happens, you must help. You will need another person, one of you to hold the mare still, the other to guide and help the foal.

There are a few mares which will just not let their foals suckle and with these, it is better to twitch them initially, so that the foal gets its first drink. After the mare realizes what it is all about, she will relax and subsequently permit it to suck.

Dress the umbilical cord with an antiseptic or antibiotic to prevent infection.

Once you have seen to everything, removed the afterbirth, seen the foal on its feet and sucking, leave the mare in peace, with a warm bran mash, some hay to nibble off the floor, and a bucket of water with the chill off it. Once daylight dawns and you can see clearly, you will need to wash the mare off with warm water, as much of the blood from the afterbirth will have clung to her tail and hind limbs.

4

Preparations
and
early foalhood

While the mare is carrying the foal, consider what amenities will be necessary for a foal. Although perfect conditions are rarely feasible, there are certain safety measures which are essential to prevent accidents.

A foal, like a child, plays hard, does not always watch where it is going and so takes tumbles. Therefore, when turning the mare and foal out, make sure that the paddock is free from barbed wire, or areas that offer a natural trap into which another possessive horse could drive the foal. No horses that are possessive or, alternatively, bossy and relish a scrap, should be in the same field as a mare and a very young foal. Although the mare will teach her foal to come to her, it will be inquisitive and may allow itself to be separated from her by either of these types.

The bottom rail or wire of a fence should not be so high that the foal can roll under it, or a sleeping foal wake up and scramble to its feet on the wrong side. Panic ensues while mare and foal rush around unable to re-unite. Watering receptacles should be safe, without any sharp edges, as foals do have a habit of pawing and then getting feet caught.

It is a common practice for young foals to be turned out with a foaling slip on to accustom them to wearing a halter, and also to make it easier for the handler to catch them. Basically, this is dangerous. Apart from the risk of the halter catching on fencing, tree limbs, or other low projections, foals in particular have a habit of scratching behind their ears and can catch a hoof in the foaling slip. So leave the halter off except at times when you will be working with the foal, or when it is in the pasture with its dam and you want to practise catching mare and foal.

Previous pages: Morgan mare and foal exercising with each other in a well-fenced paddock. This breed is exceptionally active and versatile and has a great deal of stamina.

In the stable, normal precautions should be followed. Make sure the bedding is deep enough, and pay particular attention to mucking out, which will be a lot more difficult with two sharing, particularly as a foal scampers about a lot, scattering droppings. There should be no low projections in a box, nor bucket holders fixed too low to the wall, offering a trap to hooves. Also, if buckets are placed on the floor it is best to have the handles removed. A bucket may become lodged on a hoof because the handle trapped it there. If you are going to hang haynets, only do so in a corner and tie them very high. Remember, when empty they hang a good bit lower than when full. They should not be placed lower than 1.3 m (4 ft) from the ground when empty. Hung along a wall, a haynet may be hazardous, hung in a corner it will not be in the foal's way as it moves about the box. A foal tends to rear up and put its feet over mum's back and is not particularly careful where it lands when she shakes them off. For preference, feed hay from the floor while the mare is lactating. It is a bit wasteful, but it is safe.

Early handling

The first few months of a foal's life are important, as his future will be greatly affected by how well he is cared for then. Sturdy growth; trust in people; freedom from fear of unusual happenings; general discipline; all these have their beginnings during this time, when proper care is given to his general health, and the correct approach made towards forming and developing his character, disposition and temperament.

An advantage of having a mare foal indoors is that immediate contact can be made with the foal, and its confidence in humans built up right from the beginning. If your mare is nervous with people around her

Crouching down so as not to frighten the foal by towering above it. It is important for the foal to make contact with a friendly human being right from the start.

newborn, or if she is 'foal proud', blocking your way to the foal, put a halter on her so that she can be held while attempts are made to reach the foal.

During the first few days of the foal's life it is sufficient just to work your hands lightly over his body just to accustom him to their feel. If you watch the mare caress her foal, you will see she does so along the top of his neck and this is a good place for you to copy nature. Do not approach the foal from the front and put your hand up to touch his face. Many horses dislike this and will move away, avoiding contact, and it is surprising how many people never learn this, even when the reason is explained. A horse's vision is not the same as a human's and a hand approaching its face frontally appears distorted. Approach from the side and if you wish to work towards the head do so from the shoulder. Be gentle with your movements and coaxing with your voice. If the weather is good, even if a little sharp, let the mare and foal out on the first

47

day. The sunshine will feel good to them, and the foal's long legs will benefit from the chance to stretch and carry it on its first adventurous gambols a few feet from the mare's side. For the first few days, unless the weather is really warm, limit the outings to the warmest hours of the day and also allow them the paddock to themselves. Take care which other animals are turned out with them. Gradually introduce other horses, starting with the gentlest, into their company. I owned a gelding who was a self-appointed guardian to my baby foals, keeping other horses at a safe distance, respecting the mare's domain in the field and, on occasions taking over from the mare if she temporarily forgot her foal in her haste to get back to her box and her food, shepherding the foal into its box before getting into his own.

Healthy exercise is stimulated by foals being turned out with companions of their own age and allowed to stretch their legs without restriction in the fresh air and sunshine.

Nutritional requirements

Nutrition of the mare and foal is important. Over the first few days after foaling gradually ease the mare from mashes on to the full feed she was getting previously. During the first three days the foal will be getting the colostrum that is so vital if it is to build up immunity against disease. Afterwards, the mare will be giving it the full amount of milk he needs.

Unless there is an ample supply of good grazing, the mare's feeding will have to be supplemented with hay and grain. While feeding a foal, she will need a considerable amount of hard feed as foals grow incredibly quickly, doubling their birth weight in about six weeks. After that, growth is still rapid though not so great in relation to size. However, during the first year it will attain over half its total size and weight, though most growth will be upwards and seemingly all out of proportion. If you expect to get the maximum out of your foal as a mature adult do not stint it now. The best way to start is to get the foal on to a small amount of feed as soon as possible. Even at a week old, foals can learn to nibble at grain from your hand. At first it will be from curiosity, then, relishing the taste, it will help itself from the mare's feedtub. While she has a foal at foot, and provided she is generous, feed both from one large tub on the floor so the foal can share.

If the mare is greedy, wolfs her food, or refuses to let the foal share, she can be tied up during feeding and a separate feed given in a different corner of the box for the foal. If feeding is done in the field, two containers should be provided. If possible build a creep feeder for the foal, an area fenced off from entrance by the mare but with an aperture just wide enough for the foal. It will not be long before he finds out that his personal rations are there and only he can get at them. Position the foal's feed so that the mare cannot help herself over the barrier.

The foal's general health

At about seven to nine days, on average, the mare will come into season again. This is known as the 'foal heat' and if you intend breeding from her again, you may want to send her to the stallion now, or wait till the next cycle. Foal heat sometimes makes the foal scour and he will be off-colour for a few days. If the scouring is very severe, as occasionally happens, call the vet who can alleviate the problem. Subsequent seasons do not appear to upset the foal.

Worms are an ever-present nuisance and no anthelmintic is totally effective in stopping all stages of any of the multitude of worm parasites, so a good worming programme must be maintained. From about a month old you should get the foal on to a regular programme, re-dosing every six to eight weeks. If you do see worms passed at about three weeks after dosing it means that what was at the larval stage has progressed. In this case, worm earlier, after a short interval. Occasionally vary the type of drug used, so immunities to certain drugs are not built up. Because you see no evidence in the droppings, this does not mean any animal is free of worms. Picking up droppings in pastures is a good way to help minimize the parasite burden. It also increases available grazing as horses will not eat spoilt grass. A foal that is carrying a heavy worm burden sometimes scours badly and thereby suffers a doubly debilitating hazard.

Foals should be protected against tetanus. They will have some immunity from the booster the dam was given prior to foaling, but this will not last indefinitely. The main series of injections can be started after the foal is three months old. In the USA, the schedule for 'flu and tetanus shots should be checked with your veterinarian. If left too long the foal runs the danger of being without protection. A month after the first injection a second one should be given, and a year later a booster. Thereafter he will not need another anti-tetanus shot for about three years. Your veterinary surgeon will issue the foal with a health card which is filled in each time he has an injection. It will carry the due date of the next one, to remind you.

Haltering and leading

During the first few days the foal should become used to being handled, and within a week he should be haltered and have had his first leading lessons. When putting the halter on for the first time have someone hold the mare, then work the foal into a corner so that he faces the corner with his body lined up alongside the wall. You can then effectively block his escape. Very gently work your hands over him and up towards his head, a feeling he should already be used to. Slip a rope around his neck and then ease the halter on by raising it from underneath his jaw, keeping your hands underneath. If you try putting it on with your hands over the front of his face the distortion of your hands will upset him. The natural reaction to this restraint will be to fight so be prepared to hold on to the unbuckled halter pieces, securing them as quickly as possible, meanwhile using the restraining neck rope.

At first he will fight the rope attached to the halter so make sure it is long enough to allow a bit of freeplay, so he cannot jerk free – a trick which is learnt all too quickly. Considering his small size, a foal can put up a

mighty battle at his first haltering and quite often will lose his balance and fall over. If the handler is still attached to the end of the rope when the foal gets up he soon learns that a rope means restraint and very quickly accepts the fact. If haltering is left too long the battle will be harder and the odds will become more even, and much time and confidence in the handler be lost. Horses need to get into the habit of thinking people cannot be resisted, and losing his first battle at an early age gets the foal's mind set on the right track. Firmness now will save a lot of resistances in later life, as once a horse learns he can successfully resist over any matter, it will be

Left: Teaching a foal to lead single-handed. This six-month-old Quarterhorse colt is being taught with restraint from the halter and pressure over the quarters. The handler is at the colt's shoulder and has a short lead for control. The colt is mannerly and is adapting to the handler's pace. Care should be taken not to jerk the head and neck of a very young foal. Pressure should come mainly from the rope around its quarters.

Above: Native mares and foals usually live out, but a daily handling sesson will be beneficial for the foal. This two-day-old foal will get used to being inside, a helpful preparation for the experience of being weaned.

51

Watching its dam's unalarmed acceptance of the farrier trimming her feet will help develop the foal's confidence in human beings–foals learn much by their mother's example.

very difficult to convince him otherwise. Early haltering and leading lessons set the basis for later training.

When leading initially it is no good merely pulling the halter, as the foal will not understand. Have the mare led alongside and the foal will follow. This in itself does not teach him, but every so often he will make a rush forward and be restrained by the rope.

This teaches him not to barge off. To teach him to move forward place a soft rope round his hindquarters and give a steady pull a step at a time. His reward will be the lessening of pressure from behind. Coupled with the new knowledge that he cannot barge off he will soon learn to walk in a mannerly fashion. In conjunction with the halter and rump rope you should also use verbal commands such as 'walk on' when pulling from behind, and 'stop', 'ho', 'whoa' – whichever word you choose – for him to respond to the pull of the halter rope. Use only one word or short phrase at a time, always the same one for the same requirement, and say it firmly with the same inflection each time. Many people confuse a foal (and older horses) by hiding the command amidst a meaningless, unnecessary sentence. When he complies make much of him and let your voice register pleasure. If he disobeys speak sharply with a harshly uttered 'NO'. This range of voice inflections will be very useful in later training. After a few lessons with the mare alongside, repeat them without her. Although at first the foal will resent it he has already started learning not to resist.

General handling

The foal's hooves should receive early attention, and as soon as his haltering and leading is progressing nicely the next lesson should be teaching him to pick his feet up in

the proper sequence. Use the word 'give' while holding the fetlock, pushing him slightly off-balance to facilitate picking the hoof up. He will probably try snatching it away at first, but persevere firmly, scolding if necessary. Eventually the feel of your hand, slight pressure and the word will suffice. He should also get used to having his feet picked out, and occasionally rasped. The sharp side of a rasp is too abrasive for a foal's feet so use the smoother side, and later on your farrier will be delighted to have a mannerly foal's feet to trim.

Rewarding a foal by liberal handouts of titbits can encourage nipping, especially in

A well-behaved little foal held on a webbing halter. Notice that the rope is passed through the eye and not knotted so that it will automatically tighten, rather than slip off, if the foal pulls back.

colts. Because he is young and sweet there is no reason for permitting such behaviour. Should he nip, a light smack on the side of the nose, coupled with a sharp 'NO' will surprise him and set him straight as to expected civility. It is rare for more than a couple of nips to be tried, and on subsequent occasions a verbal reprimand will often suffice. Some owners will allow their foals to nip, feeling it is unfair to chastise a baby. Teaching a colt to keep his teeth to himself ensures that as a mature stallion he will not constantly mouth at people, or worse, bite – a facet of stallion behaviour that is tolerated too often.

During the time the mare is lactating it is quite in order to continue to use her as a saddle horse, returning her to light work two or three weeks after foaling – provided the foaling went easily. At first, when being lightly ridden just to tighten her muscles up and prevent a sagging tum, the foal can run alongside. Later, you can increase her work and ride her alone. At first she will fret and call to the foal, but will soon settle down.

Many foals when first separated from their dams get frantic and can do themselves an injury, even if the box is as safe as possible, so for the first few times until you are absolutely certain that the foal is alright, have a human foal-sitter stay with him, or later on a quiet, amenable pony. If there is a playmate foal whose mum is also being ridden they will comfort each other, but in any case, at first, another person should be at hand in case of need. The top door of the box should be shut till the mare returns.

The mare should only be worked moderately and not for too long at a time, otherwise she will get fretful and her udder will be painful as the milk pressure builds. If she gets worked too hard, or is upset, it could result in a stomach upset for the foal. Some people will think it unfair to ride a mare with a foal at foot, but if she is your only riding horse there is no reason to go without a mount for the six months she is lactating. It will be easier when weaning time comes if the foal has gradually become used to mum occasionally being absent.

Left: A day-old Thoroughbred foal showing the length of leg with which foals are born, and the strong knees and hocks.

5

From weanling to two-year-old

Weaning time is one of the most unpleasant in the foal's life as he is completely separated from his dam, and at first will be very upset indeed. If he has been well handled during his first months the trauma of separation will be less hard on him than if he has not learned to trust a human being. This is why the first few months of a foal's life are so important in setting the pattern for future behaviour. The foal will transfer his dependence to the human who looks after him, in this case you, and a very strong bond of trust can be built on this basis. My Arabian stallion is a good example of this. As a foal he was extremely attached to his dam, being exceptionally shy and determined not to succumb to human advances. In the stable, he was quite easy to handle, but loose in the field he stuck to his dam and would have almost nothing to do with people. However, within a day of weaning he had completely transferred this attachment to humans and has continued to be a horse that depends to a great extent on human company. Had early handling been lacking he would have been a sadly bewildered foal indeed at his initial separation from his dam.

The first thing to decide is when to wean. No foal should be weaned until it is at least four months old, unless there is an imperative reason, such as ill health in the mare. Six months is the accepted time to wean and is generally the best for several reasons. If the mare is in foal again it will mean she will no longer needs to eat for three. If the mare is a riding horse, the owner will wish to get her back into full use without the tie of the foal. Also, at six months of age, if you live in an area with a large horse population, there will probably be several other foals in the neighbourhood going through the same rough patch in their lives, and in this instance the old adage of 'misery loves company' is very true. It will be far easier on the foal if he

can be weaned along with other youngsters, and although they will all be miserable for a short while, their unhappiness will be greatly diluted. Even though foals play hard, they will not rush around in the panic-stricken loneliness of the foal who thinks he is completely abandoned. The solitary foal risks damaging himself. Being upset, he is not aware of dangers and may crash into fences in his desire to be re-united with his dam.

Many people separate mare and foal for a short period during the day and put them back together, keeping this up for a week or so before the final break, but the better way of weaning is to make a clean break. This way the foal only has one major crisis to get through. Obviously the day chosen to wean should be one when the owner has plenty of time to cope with any situation that may arise; for most people a weekend will be best. The break must be absolute, in that mare and foal must be out of sight and hearing of each other. Therefore, it is important to make arrangements beforehand. If you have a friend who can take either foal or mare, the task will be easier, or send either to a farm or livery stable. Whether you send the mare or the foal away, make sure the place has adequate fencing around its pastures and that there are competent and responsible people in charge.

If you decide to send the mare away and you have no other horse to keep the foal company, try to get either a quiet older horse or pony as a companion, or take in another foal to lighten the load of separation for both of them. It is most important that foals have company at this time. Also, spend more time with him yourself and start forming that strong partnership which all riders and owners hope to develop with the horse they have raised from birth.

Complete separation should last a minimum of one month. During this time, the foal will learn a little self-dependence, and a lot of reliance on humans, and the mare's milk should have dried up completely. At the end of this time it is usually in order for the mare and foal to be turned back together again. However, at first keep a watch that the mare does not allow the foal to suckle. If she does, a further period is needed to dry her up completely. This may raise a storm of protest from big breeders on whose establishments things are done differently. For the owner with one foal at a time, and limited facilities,

A contented Thoroughbred mare and foal on good pasture.

it has proved successful, provided the foal is well handled before weaning, and now and then shut up while the dam is out on a ride, so it comes to accept the fact of mother coming and going without getting too fussed.

Keeping a colt entire or having him gelded

Should the foal be a colt, sometime between weaning and his second birthday the decision will have to be taken whether or not to geld him. For the majority of riders and owners, it is infinitely easier to own a gelding than a stallion, so really the only question is when to

geld. If the colt is to continue running with his dam and other horses, particularly mares, he must be done before he is a year old. Most colts do not realize their own potential till past a year, but it is possible for a younger one to get a mare in foal. However, if his other companions, if any, are geldings, it would be acceptable to leave him entire a

A Thoroughbred foal between two and three months old showing how quickly the foal's body develops in early youth. It has a very alert look, large intelligent eyes and good shoulder and pastern angles. It is safer not to leave a foaling slip on.

little longer, to mature better. It should be done soon after he is one. Veterinary surgeons prefer to geld colts either in the autumn, or before the hot weather so that afterwards the colts are not bothered by flies and the incision has a chance to heal without any infection they could carry.

If you consider keeping the colt entire, take a good look at the facilities you have for keeping a stallion, and weigh up your own capabilities for handling one; consider your reasons for wanting to keep him entire. Normally, stallions are kept by themselves, or they run with their mares; it is most unusual to find stallions or entire colts running with geldings. However, if you have enough land and facilities to keep the stallion and any other horses *safely* separated, and are prepared for the extra work involved, then the choice is yours.

Stallions are intelligent and responsive to ride. If your colt has a very good disposition and is used to a gelding's company, it would be in order to keep them together, only watch for any changes in the colt's behaviour towards the gelding. If the two have been brought up together from the colt's foalhood, the colt will probably accept his particular gelding's company. I do think it highly unfair to a stallion to be bereft of all company and to live an entirely solitary life apart from mares visiting in the stud season. However, you must have adequate facilities. Fencing must be of sound construction and horses should not be kept in an adjoining field or fights will ensue and accidents will occur whatever fencing intervenes. If space is limited and your fields adjoin each other, a double fence with a minimum of 1.8 m (6 ft) between and a height of 1.5 m (5 ft), will be required. This will be high enough to discourage jumping and far enough apart so that noses cannot touch and spark off antagonisms.

General care

Whether you stable your horses depends on your facilities. Even if they live out most of the time, they will be stabled on occasions and the mare and foal should go in separate boxes.

When the mare is out on a ride, the foal at first should have the top door of the stable kept shut, just as he did before weaning when the mare was ridden. After a while, and when he has accepted being alone, it will be safe just to shut the bottom door.

If horses other than the mare are kept it will shortly be safe to leave the foal out in the pasture with the others while his dam goes off on exercise.

As when weaning, the first few times it is important to have a friend or helper on hand, to see that all is well, but on no account should you give in to the foal who gets frantic at the mare's removal. If you do so for the sake of peace and quiet, the problem will only grow and the foal become really stupid about the whole thing. Such stupid, fractious horses are the ones that hurt themselves most often. It is always best to take a firm line, just as one would with children. Make sure no harm can come to the foal and then leave him to get over any tantrum he may throw. Each time they are separated, the parting becomes easier, until complete acceptance is reached. If he is allowed to become too dependent on his dam or another horse for company now, in later years the 'friend' syndrome will develop and your enjoyment will be greatly reduced if your horse cannot behave calmly if left alone.

During the first year of his life, the foal will achieve the greatest percentage of his growth. A yearling that will mature at around 15.2 hands and approximately 454 kg (1,000 lb) to 499 kg (1,100 lb) will already stand about 14.1 to 14.2 hands and have a weight of around

295 kg (650 lb) to 317 kg (700 lb). Naturally, he should be fed accordingly. One of the greatest mistakes that can be made with youngstock is to underfeed them. Many people feel that turning a foal out to grass till he is two or three is enough, supplementing this with hay and a little grain in winter. Unless you have absolutely prime grazing, this is not enough. The best way to feed a youngster is to feed him a working adult's ration of grain (or concentrates); and when grass is poor, or later on in the season when its nutritive quality is low, all the hay he will eat. There are alternatives, such as grass pellets, sugar beet, and the brand name cube feeds, if hay is too expensive or of poor quality, but however poor the quality, a

A Welsh Mountain Pony (Section A) mare and strong looking offspring who shows the characteristic neat head, fine tapering muzzle and big eye of the breed. Grey is the most usual coat colour. Both ponies have the high-set, gaily carried tails of their breed.

horse must have some roughage which, if grass is non-existent or very sparse, must be provided by hay.

Hand in hand with feeding go the other elements of caring for his physical well-being. Worming regularly comes top of the list. A young horse is more affected than an older one by a heavy worm burden and therefore regular dosings of an anthelmintic, prescribed by your vet, are advisable. A minimum of four times a year is essential, with very young stock preferably every two months (see page 109). Change the type of worm medicine you use periodically, and at least once a year worm for bots (see page 109).

In addition to worming, other routine veterinary care must include the continuation of the influenza and tetanus shots which should have been started as a foal.

Once the foal is on to a proper grain ration and relishes eating, you can teach him to stand tied up. A good method is to halter the foal normally, and about 0.6 m (2 ft) from the halter rope attachment, tie a piece of string long enough to reach the tie-ring. The string will withstand a considerable amount of foal pulling, but should there be a danger, it will snap. However, if the foal is tied up for his feeds every day and left for a period afterwards, he will soon accept the routine and the restraint. It is always a good idea to stay with him the first couple of times so that if he pulls backwards, he can be reprimanded and made to behave. Usually a sharp word is enough, but sometimes a tap on the rump will make him go forward and release tension on his rope. On no account tie the string to

Above: Enema of liquid paraffin being given to a young foal. Note the way in which the attendant is holding the foal with hands round either 'end'. It is important that the rubber tube on the syringe should be soft and without any sharp edges, to avoid seriously damaging the foal's rectum.

Right: Hoof showing a healthy frog, good concave sole and well put-on shoe, which fits the hoof and stops well clear of the frog. This avoids any chance of pinching and allows the frog to act normally. The nails are well seated but afford grip. It is unusual to have four nails on each side; more usual is three on the inside edge and four on the outside.

Far right: Standing quietly while tied up for the farrier, a lesson which should be taught early on. Note the quick release knot. This horse has a good open foot with a well-developed frog.

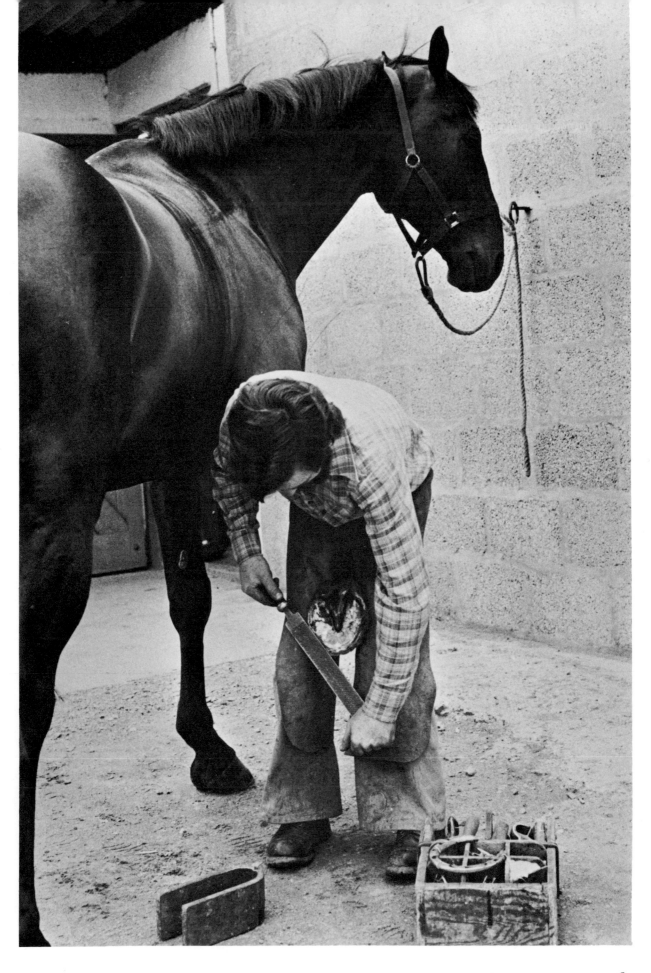

the bucket or movement of the bucket could scare the foal. If the foal chews the halter rope or string, soak it in creosote. It is also a good idea to soak rope haynets in this and then leave them outside to dry out before using them. If the tying-up lesson is left too late, the growing youngster will resist the restraint more strongly and will have the added muscle power to do so. Correspondingly stronger measures will be needed to teach him to submit.

Hoof trimming should also be done regularly and the farrier called in every two months. It is most important to have the hooves of a youngster trimmed, as during his early years his bones are soft and if the feet become uneven, excessive strain can be put on the limbs, starting problems that need not arise. If there are minor deficiencies in hoof formation, a good farrier can do a lot to encourage a better shape and angle of hoof growth.

If you are very competent with horses and learn to do the job properly, it is an economy to buy a set of nippers, a paring knife, and a hoof rasp and attend to the job yourself. Only do so if you have had proper instruction and are reasonably strong, as almost any work with youngstock requires a certain amount of strength, as youngsters can be awkward and recalcitrant. If you cannot do the job efficiently you will risk messing up both the hooves and the youngster's training, which in the end will be costly and time consuming.

Much of the youngster's handling and early training will follow directly from the first lessons learnt as a foal. Now the youngster is growing, becoming stronger, and developing a personality. During the next eighteen months much can be done to direct the foal's character along the right lines. Training can be gradually widened in scope so that when he reaches the two-year-old stage and is ready to be backed, the actual breaking process does not come as a shock, but a continuation of his earlier handling.

Many aspects of training can be accomplished, or partly accomplished, during the early years and it is never too early to teach a foal a little of the usual happenings that are part of a modern horse's life.

By weaning time he should lead in-hand very well, and once weaned, the lessons can be continued, only now, of course, he is on his own, not leading alongside his dam. Manners at this stage are all important. When a youngster is being handled, he should at all times be amenable and civil, receiving a sharp verbal reprimand when he misbehaves. Plenty of time for play when he is at liberty in the pasture. If a verbal reprimand is insufficient, it should be followed by a smart physical one, and usually one sharp tap with a whip is sufficient with the average youngster who has been firmly handled from birth. It is absolutely wrong to think that because he is young he must never be hit, as the young horse is very quick to sense when he is at an advantage. If allowed to get away with it, he will mature into an animal with a definite wilful and stubborn streak.

Many young horses, yearlings, two and three-year-olds, have never learnt to be civil to their owners, their lack of manners starting in the stable where they kick up a fuss at feed times, banging on stable doors with their forefeet; refusing to move over in the box when asked; fidgeting while being handled; being awkward about being haltered in the box; free with their teeth and heels; and devils to be caught outside. Many cannot be led in and out of a stable without barging and trying to drag the handler along, instead of measuring their speed to his. In nearly all these cases their owners are either incapable of firm discipline, or feel that because it is an animal, it has a right to push people around. Once corrected, and understanding it has to

Young stock are always better turned out in company.

behave civilly, a horse is far happier, because it knows exactly what is expected of it.

Starting with general handling, much can be accomplished during the youngster's first year. He can be taught to load quietly into a trailer or horsebox, and once loaded, to stay in till asked to come out. Other lessons include leading out in the company of an older horse to become accustomed to traffic and sights and sounds away from the normal surroundings.

It is important that the colt responds to and obeys the voice; during training sessions, use clear and concise commands, or he will get confused. Make sure the same tone of voice is used each time; the same word said in a different way will not register.

One lesson that can be learnt is to lead properly from another horse; it is surprising how many adult horses cannot do this. It is a lesson that puts no strain on a youngster and

is something that can be very useful. The first time or two, have a responsible second rider behind to keep the youngster moving forward, either by the mere fact of being there, or by a light tap on the youngster's quarters. If he is well handled and well-mannered, he will not kick.

There is no reason why a yearling cannot learn to carry a saddle and bridle, getting used to the feel of a girth being tightened and the saddle moving on his back, the stirrups swinging along his sides, and also getting used to a bit in his mouth. Provided there is absolutely nothing the bridle can get caught up on, particularly when the youngster puts his head over the stable door, it is a good thing to leave the bridle on for short periods, to accustom him to mouthing the bit, but remove the reins. For example, watch for stable doors made of vertical planks that have dried out, leaving slight gaps, where the cheek pieces could get trapped, if the youngster fidgets and rubs his head. When getting a youngster used to a girth, try on a surcingle, gradually tightening the band till the pressure is accepted and any movement made after the buckle is tightened does not frighten him. It is often the feel of the surcingle being tight when the horse moves, that makes him jumpy, not the initial act of tightening it. Later, when the saddle is introduced, it will be accepted calmly; and to get the colt used to stirrups let them hang down, but not at full length, to avoid risking a hind hoof getting trapped.

For youngsters up to two years old, lessons should be clearly given; kept very short; and not given so often that they sour the animal. This does not mean that if the youngster puts up resistances you should not persevere till you have overcome them. Nor is it necessary to teach him every day. That would be crowding an as yet unformed character and mind. General handling: haltering, leading and brushing can be on a day to day basis. The other lessons can be taken one at a time, repeating them for four or five days, then giving the youngster a week or so before continuing with something else. If you follow this system you will find you make steady progress. During the eighteen months from weaning, all the lessons should be repeated frequently, but never in lengthy sessions, as a young horse's attention span is very short. These early lessons will be the foundations for future work and the two to two-and-a-half-year-old colt will be ready to go steadily forward to the big event of being lunged and finally backed.

6

Elementary schooling

Having been well handled as a foal, yearling and early two-year-old, your youngster will drift into his early stages of schooling rather than the process coming as a shock to his system. He will be used to obeying and to learning new things and will be mentally receptive. Many virtually unhandled youngsters display resistance to early lessons.

Now you must decide whether to tackle the job yourself, or to send the youngster away to a good professional establishment. If you feel thoroughly confident that you can do the job more than adequately, recognize where you may need guidance, and are prepared to be very firm, then go ahead and school your young horse yourself.

The professional approach

If you are at all unsure of your capabilities please have the job done by a competent professional. A professional fee saved now could prove just about the most expensive bargain you ever had, as could sending a horse to a 'reasonably cheap place'.

Several months before beginning on this phase of your youngster's education make a thorough study of the facilities available at several establishments. If possible watch how horses are worked before you commit yourself to any agreement. Find out how long the initial stages of breaking will take. Anything less than a month and the job will be scrimped. The horse will either be rushed through the work, or many lessons will be omitted. It is best to do things by stages; to have the two and early three-year-old, schooling sessions broken down into two or even three sessions. For example, send the two-year-old away for a month, then when he is three, or three and a half, send him back for further schooling.

Livery and training fees vary with different establishments.

If the establishment employs good staff, they will be earning a decent salary. If only casual help is used, it is likely that your horse will be dealt with casually.

How long one spends with a young horse daily depends on how the horse reacts and progresses. Training a young horse is not merely a matter of giving him a daily lesson. Some days may indeed call for one long session, particularly if things need to be ironed out to set his mind straight. On other days, the youngster may only need fifteen minutes if he is to be put away happy and ready for progress next day.

If you decide to send your horse away, let the staff get on with the job. Nothing is more infuriating than a 'back seat trainer'. It can be extremely helpful to spend a few days at the establishment in the latter part of his training, particularly if you plan to do the furthering of his education yourself. In this time, the trainer can help fit both young horse and you together and advise you on how to progress.

Training at home

If you tackle all your young horse's training yourself the following chapters will give you a step-by-step guide to the basic education of the two, three and four-year-old horse.

A well-handled, well-fed, two-year-old will be able to start his first steps towards becoming a saddle horse either in the spring when he has just turned two, or in the autumn when he is two and a half; preferably the latter. He is a bit stronger, and can be ridden a very little, then be turned away till the following spring when stage two begins.

Most young horses' initial schooling is on the lungeline, an art requiring great concentration from the handler. It is not merely letting the horse go round in a circle. The lunge is a means of establishing discipline; of teaching and demanding obedience to verbal commands; of getting the horse to use himself and improve his stride, working him towards the day when he will be ready to accept a rider on his back.

You can tell a great deal about the horse's mental state by the look in his eye, a good guide to deciding the right moment to back him. There is no set length of time for lunging, before backing. The look in a horse's eye tells if he is enjoying his work – a relaxed frame of mind with enough brightness to make him want to put something into lessons; it warns if he is sulky and is going to give less than his best; or is feeling idle and needs waking up a bit; or is going to be a delinquent and hassle the trainer every way he can. All things will occur during the training of even the best-behaved youngster: it is not a bad thing to have a bit of a tussle on the lunge early on, get it sorted out and, consequently, the colt's mind well and truly moving along a disciplined track. A battle at this stage means that the youngster will not make any real effort to challenge the trainer later on, under saddle. A lost argument when he is very impressionable is worth ten times more than an argument later on when he is stronger, and when it might be touch and go who wins.

Some advise 'if your young horse reacts unfavourably to a lesson, stop and go back to the beginning', or 'if he is upset it is best to try tomorrow or later on', or 'he is only young and he does not understand what you want', or 'you should not chastise him because he is only young, confused, upset', and other excuses trotted out to exonerate what at times may be a very cunning animal.

It is probable that horses are far more intelligent than the charts of animal intelligence would have us believe. They can, and most definitely do, employ a modicum of reasoning power, particularly in a negative way. Many youngsters when they reach a stage in a lesson when they wish to stop co-operating, start disobeying and resent correction, appearing to become confused. If you have taken the time to study horse behaviour you will be able to see through this and decide if he is truly confused, or if he merely wishes to stop for the day. If the latter, he must be worked through his bad patch, or quite soon he will decide that any time he wishes to stop work he can act confused or upset. This also applies to the horse that never seems to be able to progress beyond a very limited point. Frequently it is the trainer's fault. If he always goes back to the beginning it is no wonder the horse very soon realizes that he only has to think to a certain point, then he can just switch off and life becomes easy. Although they can employ limited reasoning, horses have no conception of future happenings, other than the immediate ones brought on by disobedience – either a return to the start, or a reprimand which will make them realize it is better to co-operate.

Contrary to most peoples' hopes, all horses are not longing to please. They are normally content to coexist quite amicably with humans, learning a little if it interests them and costs little effort. When it becomes mentally stretching they need to be taught that co-operation is in their best interests. Your early work with your foal and yearling should have induced this frame of mind in your youngster.

Most of these aspects become evident while the young horse is having his first lessons on the lungeline. The lessons should be kept short, repeated frequently, starting with about fifteen minutes a day and progressing to thirty minutes at most, at a time. The exception is when the youngster chooses to throw a tantrum but this is not usually during the first few days, as it will be new to him and quite interesting. When it happens he absolutely must be worked through his disobedience. If he has the strength to be bad, he also has the strength to work through it till he is obedient and it is best to finish on a good note.

Lungeing method

To start a horse off on the lunge, my method is to use a leather headcollar with square brass fittings at the side of the cheeks and a brass ring fitting under the jawline. The square brass fittings should be a minimum of 2.5 cm (1 in) across. Over the nose and run through the side fittings, I run a short length of flat 1.2 cm ($\frac{1}{2}$ in) chain, one end doubled to form a loop and secured to itself, the other end run through this loop and attached to the end of the lungeline under the jaw (*see* photograph opposite). It works very much as a curb chain would, except it is over the nose, instead of merely under the jaw in the chin groove. At first glance this probably appears very severe but I have tried the cavesson method as well as the plain halter and always have had complete success with my own method, without any harm to the horse. Much more control can be achieved, and quite frequently this is needed. The horse learns that a sharp jerk means business and he very quickly gives his attention and his obedience. While he is cooperating there is no pressure whatsoever. If he makes a sudden dash forward or jerks out of his lungeing circle he brings himself up short. With a cavesson he learns that you get control gradually and he never becomes really sharp at obeying commands. With my method he learns he is under control almost instantly. For your comfort, wear cotton gloves to protect you against a rope burn caused by the lungeline being jerked roughly through your hand if the horse catches you unaware. For the horse's comfort, especially if he is an ultra-thin skinned animal and galls easily with leather equipment, wrap the leather side pieces of the halter in soft cloth until he is going easily on the lunge. At first he will sometimes pull against the restraint instead of bending into the circle. Once he learns the correct way of going, he will not be getting rubbed and padding should not be needed.

I never lunge a horse with the lungeline attached to the bit. This way the horse's mouth can be badly bruised and the tiny nerve endings gradually be dulled – the start of a hard mouth. He can also become one-sided too easily.

Absolute and instantaneous obedience on the lungeline is a very good investment for the future under saddle. The horse will be very much safer if he is used to obeying instantly, as at some stage this could prevent an accident.

To start the horse moving forward place yourself as if you were the apex of a triangle, the horse forming the base. Let the lungeline out about 2 m (6 ft), holding the excess line coiled in your left hand. With your right hand hold the lungewhip with the lash held lightly alongside the stock and gently tap the horse on the hindquarter at the same time saying 'WALK'. Take care not to be kicked if he is playful or nervous. Simultaneously take your left hand in a leading forward motion, continuing this form of encouragement till the horse moves forward. At first he will not understand about going around you in a circle which is why you have him on such a short length of line – any more and he will just turn in and face you, or you may get tangled in the excess, particularly if you are not thoroughly used to working a horse on the lungeline. A few lessons for yourself from someone competent in lungeing can be worth a lot to you and to your horse. The short line gives you control and with repeated taps and pulls he will start moving; it usually does not

take long before he is moving around you in a fair circle, a bit jerkily maybe, but at least showing that he is beginning to understand what is wanted. As soon as he is moving forward freely let your line out a little more and coax him out with the whip till he has taken up the slack. At the first lesson you should not allow him more than about 3.6 m (12 ft) of line. You must be able to reach his quarters with the tip of the lungewhip lash to keep forward movement. At this stage the movement of the lash should be soft as it is an

Starting the horse on a lunge, single-handed. The horse is wearing the equipment described in the text. Note the short rein and the hand indicating to him to walk on. The whip is about to tap the quarters and encourage movement. Restraint can be exerted over the nose but the horse is obviously happy, with one ear flicked back listening to the handler's voice. Note the handler's gloves.

indicator not a punishment. If the horse breaks into a trot during the first lesson do not worry as your prime concern now is that he understands that you want him to move in a circle around you, taking up the length of line you have allowed him.

When he has been travelling from right to left for about five minutes give a sharp command 'HO', or 'WHOA', but use the same word all the time and give a sharp tug on the lungeline. He will probably not stop at

The horse is asked to walk in a small circle by a combination of leading and lungeing, the whip pushing and encouraging him. The whip lash is held in when the horse is on a short line and is loose when he is on a long line. Here the horse understands what is asked and is walking on very freely.

first so repeat the command and the action. When he has obeyed make much of him verbally, then go towards him reeling your line in as you go. Swop your line and whip to opposite hands, turn him around and repeat the action on the other rein for the same length of time. To stop, repeat the 'HO' command and when he obeys let him stand quietly for a few seconds, then with a gentle pull on the lungeline indicate that he is to come towards you, reeling the line into the coil, at the same time as saying 'COME'. When he has reached you make much of him and lead him to his stable. Ten minutes is ample for a first lesson, as he has had several commands to think about.

Before lesson two on the lunge, here is a list of commands and the manner in which they should be used while lungeing.

Immediately before starting to move the horse should be still, not fidgeting. If he fidgets say 'STAND' firmly and sharply, accompanied by a jerk on the line if he does not. To move forwards say 'WALK', again firmly. To change gait to trot, use just that one word 'TROT' with a staccato enunciation. Later, to get canter say 'CANTER' with the word broken into two syllables with a sharp 'CAN' followed by a 'TER' which is short but less accentuated than the first syllable. For a command to stop, say 'HO' (or 'WHOA') very sharply. For the horse to come in say 'COME' in a much softer voice, as the lesson has finished, the time for orders is over and the softer 'COME' is a prelude to making a fuss of the horse. They all enjoy this end-of-lesson verbal and physical fussing. If you need to chastise the horse, always go to the horse to do so. Never make the mistake of asking the horse to come to you and then punishing him, as you will break a trust that is building up.

Other commands used in lungeing are 'WALK ON' when you want the horse to increase his stride, and 'TROT ON' for increased stride and pace at trot. A horse should not be asked to move too fast at canter on the lunge, but occasionally the same can apply for a modicum of speed with 'CANTER ON'. Many horses put their heads down during lungeing; an upwards lift of your rein hand, an indication with the whip and a 'HEAD UP' will make sure your horse does not get his down, which would bring the lungeline dangerously near his front feet. If a horse is not really using himself from behind, use the words 'TRACK UP' for a lengthening of stride at walk and/or trot, coupled with a light flick of the whip at the hind fetlocks. If the horse is rushing around too fast, jerk the line and give a sharp command 'SLOW'. If he is tending to creep upwards in speed, but otherwise is being good, say 'EASY' in a drawn out voice. Also, if he is at all nervous, upset, and going too fast, use the same 'EASY' command, with a reassuring inflection.

Short, sharp, clear commands are best understood. Do not talk to anyone watching you, as the horse will realize your attention is divided and choose that moment to pull a fast one on you.

After the first ten minute lesson when the horse merely learnt to go in a circle the real teaching process starts, establishing right from the beginning that while the horse has any form of equipment on, he is to do exactly as told – no yanking his head down for grass, no fidgeting about, and definitely no rushing around on the lunge to get the kinks out before the lesson.

Before moving on to a new gait the first one must be established. A surprising number of horses never learn to walk, either on the lunge or under saddle, but constantly break gait rather than lengthen stride and push on, at a walk. It is by far the hardest gait to teach a horse properly, as the natural inclination is to break stride upwards rather than lengthen

and speed up at walk. To achieve it the lungeline must be kept quite short at first so that every time stride is broken you can give a sharp tug and repeat 'WALK'. Watching over both the forehand and the expression on his face will tell you when the horse is about to break stride and give you just enough time to prevent it with a sharp 'WALK'. It is much better to anticipate than have to actually correct it by the punitive tug and sharp command.

For the first few lessons merely maintaining gait is sufficient. By the end of the second lesson, which can last fifteen minutes or a little more, you should be able to introduce the first strides at trot. Later on, when the horse is established in walk and trot, you can encourage more impulsion and lengthening of stride. Take things very steadily. Give him sufficient time to work, but do not overdo any lesson. Remember he is only a very young horse and should not be worked in the true sense of the word at this age. Educate by all means, but avoid too much physical stress.

At each session, work the horse on each rein to prevent him becoming one-sided. Do not always start him off on the same rein, or always follow the same pattern of ten minutes one way and switch. Sometimes do five each way and repeat, or occasionally two one way and one the other. This will prevent him becoming crafty, as some horses remember the lesson pattern, switching off when they feel it is time to finish.

As the horse becomes more proficient, lengthen the line until he is using the full length. When he has naughty spells shorten the rein so that you have more control; the longer the line the less control, but by the time he has full line stretch, he should have become very obedient to the words of command. Once walk and trot are established, start asking for extension and impulsion at these gaits. To do this, keep the horse on a line short enough so that the whip lash can just reach the hind leg nearest you. Say 'WALK ON' at the same time lightly flicking the fetlock, which will make the horse stretch that leg forward. Simultaneously indicate with the rein hand to move on by an outward movement. The horse is by now used to thinking and acting on commands and will soon recognize what you want. If you can establish this increase in stride at walk you will probably get him to increase his stride at trot by just saying 'TROT ON'.

During all lungeing work the whip plays a very important part. It has two purposes: to indicate to the horse where to place himself and when to increase stride, when it should be used with no sharp movement; and when necessary, as a punishment, when it should be used initially by cracking it back on itself (practise this first without the horse) so that the noise urges the horse to obey, or if that fails, by a sharp flick on his quarters or his lower hind leg. Only rarely will you need to use the whip frontally; this may happen with an entire colt who is angry and shows stallion tendencies to fight and answer back by threatening behaviour with his front feet or teeth. Even then, do not use it on the body but instead use the lash on the lower front legs. There is no reason to assume that an entire colt is bad tempered if when first introduced to discipline, he rebels and shows fight. It is a natural reaction, but he should not be allowed to get away with it and must be punished sharply and decisively. Once he understands that stallion aggression is intolerable to you, he will back down. If you analyse horse behaviour, most of the initial

Above left: Teaching the young horse to lunge with a helper. The helper leads him around the handler, staying on the outside.

Left: The helper encourages the horse from behind and slightly inside while he goes freely.

Above left: Walking over poles as a balancing exercise and an introduction to jumping. The handler is using his voice to encourage the horse.

Above right: The next stage, with the poles slightly raised.

Left: Learning to jump; a very small obstacle at the end of the row of poles.

resistances and tantrums are a young horse's way of weighing his chances against his or your success.

Using it as an indicator, the lungewhip can push the horse out into his circle if he starts to fall in. To do this point the whip at the shoulder and say 'OUT'. If he ignores you flick the shoulder lightly and repeat the command. Soon just an indication and the word are sufficient.

Progression to canter on the lunge should come only when he is exceptionally well behaved at walk, walk on, trot, and trot on. Any sooner and he will be breaking stride rather than trotting on and will use the canter as a means for a bit of whoopee. Speed generally excites a young horse. Cantering on the lunge helps the horse to get used to the correct lead; do not permit him to canter leading with the outside leg, but command him back to trot and then send him into canter again. Frequently, a horse will canter correctly in front but be disunited at the back. To correct this flick at the inside hind leg at the same time as saying 'LEAD'. The flick makes him switch to that leg and eventually the word is sufficient. If this fails, a momentary halt by a sharp tug to trot without the vocal command, and an immediate flick forward, back to canter usually achieves the lead change. The voice is not used in this case to bring the horse down to trot and immediately back again to canter, because only a hesitation is required, like a half halt, before forward movement is resumed. You should always establish a horse in the gait you have commanded. If you immediately change it, it confuses him and he will become very unsettled. A young horse thus unsettled in turn becomes badly disciplined and may well start to turn handler's mistakes to his own advantage.

To establish a two-year-old, a four or five-day session of lessons is necessary. Then he should have a couple of days off, and when you resume, you can work it either two on, one off; or three on, one or two off. Do this for a couple of weeks and then give him a short rest. As you are doing the training yourself there is no rush and he will benefit from easing into work. Overdoing the lungeing can make him bored and inattentive, or put a strain on him. His bones are not yet fully formed – work on a circle is more strenuous than work on a straight line; as the horse is leaning slightly inwards greater stress is borne by the inside of the feet than the outside. Lungeing teaches him to be supple and to use his hindquarters.

Lungeing tacked up

Once reasonably proficient at lungeing, introduce a surcingle to get the horse used to girth tension; (see page 66) the next step is to place a large sack – much larger than a saddle pad – under the surcingle so that it can flap as you lunge the horse. This helps break down any fears the horse may have; accidents are often caused by horses being frightened by little things.

The next stage is to lunge with saddle and bridle on. Fit a snaffle bridle on under the lungeing headcollar and make it comfortable. The saddle should be girthed snugly; caution should be used when tightening the girth if the horse is unaccustomed to this, as he may panic and buck or shoot forward. The stirrups should at first be knotted up so that they will not slip down when the horse is moving. At first, the horse will probably be upset by the feel of the restricting girth as he moves. When lungeing the apprehension will show in his eyes and in the way his back bunches and his stride becomes jumpy and short. At walk he will soon settle, but at the trot, with each diagonal moving, the saddle will move on his back. This may cause him to buck very

slightly, rather like little crow hops. If this is all, speak reassuringly to him. If, however, bad temper (and by now you should know your horse well enough to distinguish naughtiness from fear) results in a good buck, a very sharp jerk and a 'BEHAVE' will register. Sometimes only a few bucks are put in and he will settle down, yet other horses just show slight apprehension and then realize no harm is being done. Most, fortunately, do the latter, especially those that have been well handled.

After getting the horse used to the saddle and bridle, let the stirrups down so they are swinging against his sides. If you normally ride very long take the stirrups up a few notches to avoid risking a hoof getting caught in the iron. While the stirrups are down put the horse through all gaits, especially canter as it is at this gait that he will move most. He

A horse at a more advanced stage of training, lungeing well, with a good head carriage and bend, and at the stage where it can wear side reins without interfering with its balance. Initially it is better for the young horse to be lunged without side-reins so that it can use its head and neck to balance itself and learn self-carriage.

should he get used to loose, flapping irons without spooking, so they do not make him panic if his rider falls off.

Backing

The next step from lungeing with tack on, is to climb aboard for the first time. The eye of the horse is the guide as to how he is feeling and this is the 'green light' for the right day for first mounting. During lungeing sessions you will have observed a wide range of emotions and feelings; when you know the

A horse moving freely on the lunge. Note the rider has no reins and cannot interfere with the horse's mouth but has stirrups to maintain balance, if for any reason the horse should shy.

horse is relaxed, calm and receptive, that is the day to ask him to accept your weight for the first time. You must have someone else present. You will need help, from a safety angle and to reassure the horse that all is well.

Although the horse has now reached the stage to be backed and ridden, it is still good practice to give the first part of his lessons on the lungeline. This will help settle him and until he has been ridden at walk and trot and is calm about the whole thing, lungeing should continue as part of his work. Periodically throughout his training, lungeing will be beneficial.

As a preliminary to mounting, take the lunging headcollar off and substitute an ordinary one over the bridle, but with the reins outside, so that the halter does not restrict rein movement. The horse should not be held by the bridle rein, because if he moves suddenly he gets a jab in the mouth from the restraining handler and may associate mounting with discomfort. Have a handler standing at the right-hand side of the horse's head holding him on a very short length of leadrope. With his free hand he should hold the off stirrup so that the saddle does not go askew when your weight is put in the nearside stirrup. At first merely gather the reins with minimal feel on them, then place your foot in the stirrup and raise yourself up. Repeat this a few times, and if the horse is calm, proceed to rest your weight across his back but with your foot free of the stirrup once up there. This is all you need to do at the first session. The follow-on is to repeat this and then to stand up above the horse's back with all your weight in the left stirrup. It is often the height of the rider above him that causes the horse concern, so repeat this a few times before swinging your right leg across his back and gently lowering yourself into the saddle. The handler at his head should at the same time speak reassuringly to him. Once seated in the saddle speak to the horse, again reassuringly, and if he is calm proceed to move around in the saddle and to feel him behind the cantle with one hand. A few mountings are all you should attempt at the first try.

The next stage is to mount and to get the horse to move under you. You will still need the second person for a couple more days. At first do not touch the horse with your legs but say 'WALK ON' as the handler starts to lead the horse forward. He should do this very slowly; it is often the actual first few movements with a rider aboard that spook a horse, rather than the mere fact of a rider sitting there while he stands still. Have him led around your arena on both reins. Ten minutes of this is enough for the first try. On the second day, repeat the exercise, but let the horse feel your legs lightly squeezing as you say 'WALK ON'.

When you feel he is very calm, probably on the third day, try going solo but still have a handler around in case of confusion. The horse should have learnt the commands to 'WALK' and 'HO' thoroughly on the lunge and be able to interpret them with a rider on top. Bring your legs on to his sides as you give him the verbal command and take them off when he complies. At first, without the help of a person on foot, the horse will be very unsure of himself and not know he has to walk around the arena, but by using what is termed an open hand or leading hand you should be able to turn him to left or right and his front end will move, even if his back end does not. To do this you move your left hand out from his withers so he can see the hand movement, somewhat like leading him. The

action of pulling his forehand around will pull him off balance and get him started, after a few tries, if not at once. Do not worry if he appears to wander aimlessly at first. The main thing is that he moves forward, the direction does not matter. Provided your groundwork on the lunge has been thoroughly instilled into him you will find that he very quickly gets the message and after about ten or fifteen minutes he will be making a more or less adequate circulation of the arena. When this is achieved try stopping him a few times using 'HO'.

A fifteen minute lesson under saddle at this stage is plenty. Give him a three or four day spell of just walking with plenty of halts, turns, and very large circles on both reins so that he learns to cope with carrying a rider and balancing himself well, and also learns to recognize the leg and hand aids when coupled with verbal commands. When he seems to be responding, try omitting the verbal commands to see if he now understands the leg and hand aids by themselves.

After establishing walk and stop and turns give the horse a few days break before proceeding to trot. A young horse comes back mentally fresh and much more receptive after a mini-break.

Getting the horse to trot for the first time will need considerable verbal encouragement and a little more forceful use of your legs as he will only want to take a few steps before coming back to walk. Encourage briskly with voice and legs to maintain forward trot and after about 50 m (50 yds) let him walk again, repeating the exercise till he feels more confident and starts coping with the arena bends adequately. At this stage a young horse is still very unsure of moving forward freely with a weight on his back, and at the trot even more so than at a walk.

Do not ask a really young horse to progress beyond the trot stage, particularly if you have the opportunity to educate him gradually. Instead, try to establish him well in walk and trot, get him reasonably supple and going forward calmly under arena conditions. Never, ever, make the mistake of having him on a very firm rein. You need that mouth as soft as possible and should use only the very lightest of contact. Firm contact will prevent him moving forward freely, indicate insecurity on your part, and will make him think that control is via the mouth, whereas the real control should come from careful groundwork and the trust building up – not that your reins should flap, but neither should they be held firmly. Too few horses have really good mouths; too many of them lean on the bit while their riders fondly think they are on a contact.

Many horses, even those supposedly well schooled, fail to back up really well, resisting with their mouths, putting their heads up and hollowing the neck in front of the withers. For ease of handling, your youngster must be able to back up adequately, without resentment or resistance. The movement should first be taught on the ground, preferably with the lungeing headcollar on, rather than a bit. Stand in front of the horse and push away from you with the headcollar with your left hand; with your right hand use the butt end of a dressage whip to press into the horse's chest. Simultaneously say 'BACK' and repeat the word for every stride you want. If the horse resists persist at first with the same method. If he is obviously not prepared to listen give him a sharp rap across the chest at the same time as repeating the halter pressure and command. When he fully understands the command and will back merely for the verbal order is the time to try it under saddle. It is best to try it alongside a fence to help keep him straight. Use the verbal command, apply firm but not dead pressure to both reins and ask him to come back to you.

At first do not use leg pressure. He is still very green and may get confused. Only ask for one step at a time, then release the pressure, pause and ask for another step. If necessary, use a person on foot at first to help. When he is complying well, bring your legs on to his sides, and at this stage you can also start asking him to keep his body straight with leg aids. Later on much more refinement can be achieved with backing up, but for a green, barely broken horse this is adequate.

After two or three sessions, each lasting four or five days, interspersed with about a week's break, it is a good idea to introduce him to going out for his first ride; at a walk and definitely in the company of a tried and trusted steady horse or pony. He will learn a tremendous amount from his first companion on the trail. If that companion is steady and used to his job your youngster will copy. If he is stupid and flighty, the young horse will be quite likely to follow this example. Never excuse bad behaviour on the grounds of youth. If he is properly and steadily trained he will never have occasion to pull a bad fit, and even a minor one should be dealt with very firmly right at the start. Badly-mannered and permissively excused young horses turn into dangerous and uncivil older animals.

Once your two-year-old gets up to this standard you can do one of three things. You can trickle him over the next six to eight months with a very little work; you can elect to give him a complete break for a couple of months, repeat the lessons, then give another break; or, if he has been backed in the late autumn, you can let him winter without any more work and bring him up as a three-year-old, when furthering his education can be more progressive and more regular riding can be achieved. The latter is best. He has been taught civility before he gets set in his ways mentally, or strong enough physically, to argue. At three, a week's groundwork and a

few refresher lessons will set him fair to real progress. If you decide occasionally to ride your rising three-year-old, on no account must he be really *worked*. He is still a baby, several years off maturity. A gentle walk and trot, for a half-hour maximum, once or twice a week is enough, provided he is quiet. If he is too lively turn him away completely as you will have to work him too much to achieve required calmness. It can wait till he is three or three and a half years old.

A good exercise for both horses and riders is to work sometimes in pairs, particularly to school a young horse with an older one – here, father and son. Nearer to the camera is the sire, going in a more collected manner, on the bit, with an educated head carriage, while the younger horse shows more interest in the countryside around him.

7

The three-year-old: early riding

The expression on a horse's face gives a good indication of its character. This three-year-old Morgan is alert and good-natured, with the wide brow, generous eye and refined head characteristic of the breed.

Teaching a young horse to lead quietly and calmly into a trailer or horsebox should be done with care. Here the trailer has been carefully positioned so that the wall of the barn and the line held by the helper provide an enclosed area.

Right: Here the youngster is gently but firmly encouraged.

Centre: Matting on the ramp provides a firm footing; and a titbit can help.

Below left: The front ramp has also been let down to make the inside of the trailer lighter and less tunnel-like. The lunge line is used to encourage from behind.

Below right: Being able to see the other horse already inside the trailer helps to reassure the youngster.

Springtime is the ideal time to start the second stage of education as a saddle horse. The ground has dried out ensuring there is no undue pull on tendons and muscles, and when there is no sharpness in the air your young horse is less likely to be coltish when asked to return to work.

Your youngster will have had all winter to grow; you will see a tremendous change in his physical appearance. He will have stopped the erratic upward growth characteristic of yearlings and two-year-olds. He will have begun to flesh out, appear rounder and heavier, with his muscles beginning to show. The depth through girth and barrel will show a marked difference. The chest development and also the muscles on the inside of his thighs, will be more marked – a horse that tends to 'brush' at two, three and four may well grow out of this as he matures and muscles up.

He is now ready to progress from the very basic stages of his education to the stage where he can give you a pleasant ride. But do not make the mistake of hurrying him. He is still developing physically and mentally and this year in his life should really mould him into a potentially good saddle horse.

His previous education will have consisted of lungeing and being backed and walked and trotted quietly on home territory with one or two short outings in the company of an older steady horse. Begin by going over all the lessons learnt the previous autumn, starting with two or three days lungeing, followed by a very quiet and unhurried re-introduction to being ridden. Initially, he will probably be unsure of himself but if his former lessons were not skimped, he will settle into the old work and be ready to learn more. His two-year-old performance will have been very basic; all that should have been achieved is a mannerly horse, willing to walk and trot forward, and halt and back up on command,

wearing a snaffle bridle. As a three-year-old you can polish his performance and if necessary, give further thought to bitting.

Most horses are ridden in a simple jointed snaffle. Many go well with this bit. Others go abominably and get into the habit of leaning heavily on the rider's hands. It is often best to take a horse out of a snaffle bridle if he shows any tendency to lean on it. It is tedious to fight a horse that gets heavy on the forehand and changing to a mild action Pelham, mullen mouth with medium shank below the bit and short shank above, gives a much lighter communication with the horse; he learns to respect the potential power of a curb without your needing to use the bit's strength, except initially, to advise him co-operation is best. He ends up with a much more responsive mouth, is usually better balanced and does not travel on the forehand. Having him in a curb and learning to respect it is infinitely better than having him heavy in your hand and unable to progress to a more refined performance.

If you choose to change from a snaffle to any bit with potentially stronger action, please first consider how good or bad your own hands are. A tendency to lean may be created by insufficient use of seat and legs or other bad riding habits. It can be helpful to consult an instructor who may suggest improvements in the way you ride.

Many horses never learn to travel straight. Others are very fidgety with bits, or persistently resist bit pressure. If you had taken your young horse up on to firm contact, you would have laid the foundations of a very real resistance problem and also prevented him from moving strongly forward. With the latter case, forward impulsion being lost, the horse could resist the contact by going sideways, which he would mentally equate with avoiding bit pressure.

Lengthening stride at walk and trot

Spend considerable time on the walk and trot, getting the young horse to use himself at these gaits and to come back in his downward transitions smoothly and rapidly, before attempting to teach him to canter. Speed can come later. It is much more important to teach obedience first. Restraint should not just be via the bit, which should only be used as an indication of what you want, not as the sole means of achieving it. At this stage concentrate on your youngster learning to walk on, really using his hindquarters and getting his hocks underneath him to develop a good long stride. Most horses have a bad walk, ambling along with absolutely no impulsion from behind. When greater speed is required they usually break into a sloppy jog. Most riders have no idea how to elicit a really good walk from their horses, although they may have achieved a very passable series of sitting, working and extended trots, and hand, working and extended canters.

Developing a good walk on a horse is the foundation for all the other gaits. It teaches him that he must use himself within the gait he is already travelling at; his hindquarters become very active; his stride lengthens; he will be more up together – not exactly on the bit in the accepted sense, as only a modicum of contact should be used, so light as to be almost non-existent. If you have to rely on strong pressure from the front to restrain a horse he will not learn to drive forward, because he will interpret bit restraint as a check and not comply with the verbal and physical urging of his rider to walk on; so will drop back to a slower gait, with markedly less impulsion. However, some bit restraint is necessary to teach the horse not to break gait unless asked to do so. When teaching the horse to really walk out, bring your legs on to his sides and squeeze him forward saying 'WALK

ON' firmly. At first he will tend to break gait and go into a trot. Do not wait for him to break gait, you should be able to anticipate it. Take a light but firm hold with the rein, at the same time keeping your legs on and re-iterating the 'WALK ON' command. In effect your legs are saying 'GO ON' while your hands say 'DON'T BREAK GAIT'.

Before long response will be forthcoming from the leg pressure, without the need for restraint from the hands. Earlier work on the lunge will have taught the horse to stride out at walk and trot, so it will be easier under saddle. Do remember that when the horse is walking his head moves back and forth so your hands should also move back and forth by the same amount. If you fix your hands at walk the horse will either slow down or stop. Even if you are riding on a relatively loose rein the hand should not be fixed, as the weight of the rein on the bit is enough to cause pressure on a horse with a good mouth. At the trot, however, the horse's head is still and your hands should be too, only keeping a light feel on the mouth, not a firm contact.

Virtually the same system can be used for teaching the horse to lengthen stride at the trot when no increase of pace is required. If he finds restraint from the front while your legs still ask for more he will lengthen stride without speeding up. However, remember at both gaits to take the leg pressure off once you have achieved the required length of stride or speed, or he will be confused. Immediately he slackens, bring the pressure back, but only for as long as it takes. If you have an idle horse that just will not tune in to lesson time and who appears to have very dull sides, then it is quite in order to give him a sharp switch behind the girth. It is much better to do this than constantly to push and prod. That will only teach him that he can ignore your demands, and in time he will get permanently dull sides and also a dull mind.

Carry a dressage whip when schooling because it is long enough to reach behind the saddle without moving your hand position and thin enough to register when used sharply, where a thick crop or cane tends to be duller in effect and is capable of bruising. A dressage whip can also be used as an extra directional aid when teaching the horse to yield to the leg in more advanced movement.

Arabian stallion at an extended trot. He is being ridden in a Pelham, which, provided the rider has good light hands, will discourage him from leaning on the forehand.

The importance of leg and hand aids

The horse must not only be taught to move forward with impulsion and a really good stride, but also that the legs and hands can place him in many positions. Although he may naturally travel straight, he may find it difficult as a youngster when he has a rider aboard. Very few riders sit absolutely perfectly. The horse may be inclined to travel crooked, or he may be one-sided – more supple on one rein than the other. He will also find it awkward at first to bend himself properly round corners and to describe a good circle.

At this stage you should teach him really to respond to your legs in positioning himself, and in bending his body in a good arc when turning. Start this at the walk, when riding in the arena. On coming to the corners, use the inside leg with a very definite pushing movement slightly behind the girth where the rib cage is prominent. This will have the effect of pushing the hindquarters away from the leg and into the arc desired. Later, you can lessen the pressure and the leg can be less far back, until you reach the stage when the horse will automatically bend into corners and requires only an occasional minimal leg aid. The hands, meanwhile, should be held quiet, as at this teaching stage, usually only the hindquarters come into the inside of the track. If you find the horse falls in completely to the inside of the track, then the outside hand pressure can indicate he must stay to the outside of the track and the inside hand can also help, with a lateral pressure. Repeat this exercise at the trot. The basis of horse training is all a system of pressures of varying degree and different placements, and the horse's reward for compliance is the ceasing or decreasing of pressure.

To help supple him and teach him to bend continuously, ride him in large circles, on both reins, at walk and trot; at the same time engaging his hindquarters. Take care that he does bend. Many riders when executing large circles in fact let the horse do a series of rather short straight lines with no smoothness of movement or curvature of the horse's spine. The horse should be describing a very gradual arc the whole time he is circling. This will be a progression from pushing him into and around his corners. At the same time that your inside leg is indicating to him to keep his quarters out on the arced track, your outside leg will hold him from swinging his quarters too wide.

He should have had enough basic schooling on the lunge and on the straight not to require constant pressure for forward movement. If he does lag, push forward with both legs, resuming the inside leg pressure to keep his quarters away from arcing out. Your hands need to be steady, but as he is in a continuous turn the inside part of the bit will have very slight turning pressure from the rein the whole time. The outside rein will maintain minimal contact unless the horse tends to lean in with his shoulder, neck and head. To counteract this use a slight holding resistance to the outside, maintaining the turning pressure to the inside of the circle.

When the horse is capable of gradual large circles, decrease the size of the circle, but maintain the same good walk or trot. The horse will find it harder to increase his bend and stabilize his gait. The aids for turning will need to be correspondingly stronger and the impulsion from behind greater, therefore the leg aids must be very positive. Once circling well, change the format and describe figure eights, making sure the horse changes his bend from nose to tail. For variety, ride large serpentines. If you constantly do the same exercise the horse starts to anticipate and gets careless, or becomes bored. No exercise should be done to excess unless the horse really is in an uncooperative mood, (*see* page 69).

As with initial schooling, do not overdo lesson sessions. Three or four days at a time should always be followed by at least one day off, preferably two. A system of one day on, one off is not as good as the horse does not get into the swing of it. Let him learn a little well, then rest; he will come back much fresher and be ready to absorb new lessons more willingly.

Do not sour the horse by never-ending repetition of the same exercise. Vary the lessons. Keep them to thirty minutes or a maximum of forty minutes, without flitting from one thing to another every few minutes. Let the horse work at one move for a short period before moving on to something else. Strike a happy medium of enough consistent work to get the horse co-operating and using himself in one gait, before changing up or down a gait. Work on your bending and circles, etc., for a few minutes, then straighten out and use the whole arena. Do individual circles or serpentines, then straighten out once more. In other words, vary the actual demands while still keeping the whole lesson within the framework of the work he is learning at the moment.

To broaden his outlook, take him on short hacks, at first with a companion; once he has settled, by himself. Use only the walk and trot and keep the speed well within immediate control. As he develops confidence take him to new places, introduce him to a variety of things, initially using the companion to instil confidence. Walk him through water, mud, over bridges, and through streams. Quite often sunlight on water will spook a horse and he will need reassurance. A horse will sometimes walk through a wide stretch of water and resist puddles by curving around them. Here is where your work with hand and leg, keeping

him straight, will pay off. A horse ridden only from the front and used to rein control will be able to evade commands by going crabwise. It is very important to have control of the horse's hindquarters at all times, as often you may be able to pull a horse's front end out of trouble but if he knows he can resist leg aids to move to the side, he could endanger both of you sometime, spooking out from a hedge into traffic.

Shying

A horse's ears are a good guide to spooking or shying. If he is relaxed, his ears may be at 'half mast', neither back nor straight forward. If he is relaxed but interested, he will have them pricked forward, but still be moving on strongly. If he is disturbed at all he may prick them, but his gait will become hesitant. Reassure him and push him on. If he is being plain silly, also growl at him – the disapproving voice can often get through to him better than stronger aids, as one often gets to the point of running out of push. If his ears are very pricked and he is looking to one side or the other, curving his neck and body away from the direction his ears are pointing to, it is often the beginnings of a shy. Many horses will warn their riders this way if the riders take the trouble to recognize it. This type of shying can be corrected by applying opposing aids and vocal reprimand. If you have to use a whip to correct a stupidly shying horse do not strike him behind the saddle, which will make him move forward, but either on the neck or shoulder as he tenses to jump sideways. This has the effect of his encountering trouble from the side he least expected it, and provided it is sharp enough, will deter him from jumping away from the 'maybe fear' into the 'positive punishment'. Later on only the voice will be needed. If you ignore warning signs and always reassure and pacify the horse he will realize that shying can be quite diverting and a vice can be started in him. This is different from the genuine fears, of which there are relatively few.

The other type of shying is that in which the horse gives no warning, and literally jumps sideways away from whatever is scaring him. It could be something as innocuous as a leaf, or a bird fluttering in the bushes. When this happens it is no cause at all for reassurance or he will go on shying at such silly things. Very quick reaction on the rider's part is needed, coupled with extremely sharp restraint via bit and leg to stop a surge forward and to push his body back into the line he diverted from. If he persists in such behaviour, a pattern will be set which the rider can detect, counteract, and if necessary punish by both voice and whip.

My stallion Nizzolan has always seen bogeys at every log and as a youngster used them as excuses to pretend fright. Now as an older horse, he still tries to convince me that bogeys live in logs, but he always announces he is going to shy and a sharp command of 'DON'T YOU DARE' makes him go by without doing anything. On other occasions, if he is annoyed at being restrained to a slower pace than he wants, he works out that he will answer back by reacting to anything that looks shyable, again announcing in advance. If I had let this go unheeded as a youngster it could now be a dangerous habit. Instead, it is just his way of mildly having the last word, or almost the last.

Teaching general manoeuvrability

Once the horse is responding to leg aids for forward and lateral movements, it can be useful to teach movements not normally included at this stage. These are: turns on the forehand, turns on the haunches and a complete side-pass, as opposed to a half or full-

pass. These are valuable movements for him to know while out riding, for opening a gate, for instance – and closing it in a restricted area, using your left hand to open the latch while moving from right to left, or vice-versa. These movements enable you to open gates fully, instead of being barged through them half open, which may cause a nasty accident if the horse has not been taught to co-operate.

Neck-reining

A horse should be able to be ridden with one hand and respond to neck-reining, or as it is termed in English riding, the indirect rein. This can be taught while the horse is learning to bend into his circles by using the direct feel on the inside of the mouth and the indirect feel of the rein on the opposite side of his neck, just in front of the withers. He will respond before long by bending away from the indirect rein aid. To teach him really to neck-rein, use the direct inside hand aid, the indirect aid on the opposite side coupled with the outside leg pushing on to his side just behind the girth. As mentioned previously, training is a series of pressures. The horse will move away from the pressures of indirect hand and leg and before long you will get him to turn independent of the bit, relying only on indirect rein and outside leg. Coupled with the ability to place his body in any position you need by use of your legs and light bit aids, you will be able to use this talent to ride one-handed for a variety of needs, one of which is opening a gate. Purists may say one should always ride with two hands, but there are many occasions when it is necessary to have one hand free.

Above right: A young horse very obediently standing quietly while the rider opens the gate.

Below right: The horse moving right up to the gate from the rider's left leg while he closes the gate.

92

Turn on the forehand

Initially it is easiest to teach this with the horse halted alongside the arena fence, with his body not far away from it. Lightly feel his mouth and for a turn to the left bring your left leg on to his side just about 15 cm (6 in) behind the girth giving a little steady pressure with the left rein – not enough to turn his head as for a normal turn but just a feel to incline it around. At first he will probably move forward, but you should restrain him steadily with the right hand, while still asking with the left hand and leg. Aligning him with a fence limits the turn to 180 degrees but helps place him better. At first his turns on the forehand will be very ragged, but provided he moves away from the leg, moving his hindquarters in a large circle and his front legs in a small circle, obeying the left rein, sufficient has been achieved. Reward him vocally, walk on, halt and repeat the movement to the opposite direction. It will not be long before the movement becomes less ragged and a cadence with front and hind legs will begin to show. When the horse is achieving passable turns by the fence, take him into the middle of the arena and repeat the request. Without the fence guideline it will be less easy, but he will know what the aids mean and be able to co-operate, and also be able to describe a full 360 degrees. With a Western-trained horse complete immobility of the forehand is essential apart from the hooves pivoting on the spot.

Turn on the haunches

This is the opposite to the turn on the forehand. The front end describes the large circle and the hindquarters the smaller one, all in a rhythmic cadence. The aids used to teach this are: to turn to the left, take a feel on the left side of the mouth with a slightly open hand leading away from the withers.

Place the right leg on the girth, or just in front of the rear part of the shoulder and press laterally. The inside, or left, leg, holds the horse in place by preventing him backing up. If he tries to walk forward, resist with the right rein, immediately going back to the open hand left rein for movement to the left. Most young horses make the mistake of trying to turn around normally and you have to be pretty subtle about preventing forward movement and about holding the hindquarters relatively still while asking the horse to move his forehand in a large circle. As with the turn on the forehand, start this move alongside the fence. Use the turn on the haunches as a preliminary to getting a Western-trained horse up to 'spins'.

Side pass

This is a very useful move in which the horse only moves laterally, with no forward motion at all. It is not easy for the horse, but once taught, demonstrates just how well the horse obeys hand and leg. As well as moving sideways, the horse must keep his body straight and the tendency is for him to move it in a slant. Initial aids for this are: a holding with the reins, coupled with holding the opposing rein alongside his neck and a slightly open feel on the right side of the bit for a move to the right. Your right leg remains passive, ready to hold the horse in place should he move backwards, and your left leg closes strongly on his left side, pushing sideways. It is an impressive movement when well accomplished and is called for in many Western trail classes, where it has to be done with neck-reining and leg aids. It is useful in day to day riding with English-trained horses, to move a horse alongside an object, or to open a gate, coupled with a turn on the forehand. It is also very handy having a horse that will definitely move away from the opposing leg, (*see* Shying, page 91).

For the above three movements the aids need to be rather exaggerated at first but as the horse becomes proficient, they should be minimal and hardly discernible.

The canter

It is better for a horse to be very manageable and very obedient to hand and leg, before he is asked for additional speed. Speed excites a horse and excitement is the last thing needed in a youngster. Therefore plenty of work should precede the canter to stabilize him and get him obedient to the controls.

A good plan is to revert to the lunge for a few days, concentrating on the canter and employing the voice extensively, so that the horse positively links the movement with the word. When you subsequently try it on his back, you will not need such strong aids to send him into the canter and he will be already reasonably well balanced in the gait, better able to cope with the transition from trot to canter and to maintain the canter without having to change down through insecurity.

For the first few times cantering, use an area large enough so that cornering presents no problem and do not worry about the correct lead yet. That will come later. Have him trotting slowly, take a very light feel on the reins and close your legs on his sides without actually pressuring him. This will tell him that he is to do nothing yet, but that some new command is going to come and will alert him to pay attention. After a few strides squeeze with both legs and at the same time say 'CANTER' clearly. Do not let him speed up at the trot. Many horses, supposedly trained, do this and it is the wrong way to teach a youngster. All he learns is that he is allowed to hammer on at trot till he can go no faster and then he breaks into a canter. This is not obeying any command, rather the reverse. Work the horse on both reins and once he is confident about his transitions it is time to start teaching him his correct leads.

Many horses never learn to canter on a given leg and many remain hard-gaited on one lead, switching to the smoother one if the rider is not attentive. This is usually the result of being allowed to become set in their ways, with no actual schooling done on leads when young. After two or three sessions cantering, when he knows what you want as far as the gait is concerned, start sorting your youngster's leads out.

Start a youngster off in canter on a corner, so that it is easier to drop him on to the required lead. Unless a horse is almost a natural, the generally accepted method does not usually work as well as this one. A horse cantering to the left should be striking off with the off-hind, followed by the near-fore, but to all appearances it is the near-fore that is the obvious leading leg, which is why it is called 'leading with the near-fore'. If your horse is a natural and is not inclined to pick up incorrect leads, the aids should be a light feel on both reins, a closing of the legs, then a minimally stronger feel on the inside rein, closing your outside leg just behind the girth and a squeeze forward with your inside leg. This has the effect of bending the horse in the direction you are going, while your right leg says 'pick up your off-hind' and the squeeze asks for impulsion. The three movements are hard to synchronize but this is what gets the transition, so concentrate on them and make sure that you can merge them together, if you expect your horse to comply.

Another method with a horse that is not a natural on his leads is to follow the above method with the legs, but with the hands, slightly incline his head away from the direction in which he is travelling. The leg and hand aids MUST be synchronized for maximum efficiency. This has the effect of

A three-year-old Quarterhorse filly, recently broken-in.
Her canter shows fluid movement with good impulsion.
She is being ridden on very light contact and holds her
head slightly high but overall is going very well for such
a young horse.

cramping the outside foreleg and freeing the inside foreleg, for him to move forwards. If your horse is having difficulty picking up the correct lead, make sure your weight is on your outside seatbone as you give the canter signal. The head should not be turned much, you will then be able to correct the bend easily; and once the horse has become established in right and left leads, both on the corners and on the straight. When a horse is very good at canter from trot and later from walk and even halt, taking the requested lead, you should be able to signal him merely by brushing on his side with your outside leg. As at the walk, the horse's head in canter moves back and forth, so sympathetic hands are essential.

After the horse has become clever with his leads, take him a stage further and teach him to change leads on command. As a three-year-old it will be sufficient to teach a simple change and this is most effectively done in a figure eight. He should be used to cantering in large circles and his transitions should be smooth, with no tendency to become excited. Use the greater portion of the arena, or all of it, if a small one. Trot your figure eight first, noting where you come off the track to go across the arena. Then put the horse into a canter and as you come off the track, bring the horse down to trot across the diagonal part of the arena picking up the opposite lead as you hit the track at the other side. Practise this on both reins till the horse is correct each time. Gradually lessen the number of strides between each change of lead until all that is needed is one or two strides. At no time permit the horse to anticipate or get excited, common faults when teaching this move. If this happens, start again calmly and take more strides at trot, to calm the horse.

The point made about leg pressure is also relevant to the various other moves discussed in this chapter. When the horse is really schooled and very light to the aids, you should be able almost to dispense with pressures, substituting merely an indication through the rein and a minimal signal from your legs. Making heavy weather of the aids makes for a horse rather heavy in the hand and dull in the sides. If at any time the horse seems to switch off and requires repeated pressures from you during lessons, stop and think. Extra and increased pressure will dull him, and make him realize that switching off means he can have a mental rest and give a poor physical performance. Judicious use of your dressage whip to recall him to duty is far better and kinder to him than dulling his mouth and sides with heavy pull and push.

Broadly speaking a tap behind the girth means forward or away movement (depending on the indication of legs) and a tap on the shoulder should help to control the front end. With the first he is moving away from the whip; with the second he is moving into it. If you want a horse to move his forehand around and he is resisting, it is no good switching him behind. Tapping his shoulder will register, coupled with the aids.

If you can teach your horse all or most of the foregoing over a period of a few weeks, it will be plenty for a three-year-old to digest. Then give him a rest. Caution should be exercised, however, to make sure the horse is not being confused or unduly resistant. If such a situation arises seek good professional help immediately. During his training do give him fun days of hacking, but even then, do not let him amble along; always ask him to perform in the manner he has been taught. The fact that he is away from the lesson arena will be refreshing, and any demands you make on him will convince him that being on the trail does not mean behaving sloppily, or getting jazzed up. Many horses are badly behaved on a hack, jigging, going crabwise, head tossing and bumbling along on their favoured lead, sometimes even disunited. All this makes hacking less pleasurable for the rider. They are not corrected because they are not being schooled at the time. Arena schooling should aim to make the horse an enjoyable ride; schooling merely for its own sake is pointless.

Throughout this year do not make the mistake of rushing or hurrying your very young horse. Give him a chance to develop. After a few weeks of working him into the second stage of his education, give him a complete holiday. If possible turn him away for the summer – he is still growing physically. Autumn will be early enough to refresh his memory, and during the winter you will be able to ride him very lightly for about an hour at a time provided no stress is involved. Keep to light hacking, while incorporating tuition. From autumn onwards give several periods of a few weeks when the horse is not ridden at all. When spring comes round again he will be ready to advance into his adult life.

A three-year-old Thoroughbred turned out in winter to exercise himself. Note the excellent solid fencing. A Thoroughbred should be stabled at night in late autumn and winter. He will be growing, and during a rest period in winter will need unlimited hay day and night and two concentrate feeds daily. This youngster is wearing boots to support the tendons and to prevent him knocking himself while galloping round in play.

8
The four-year-old: starting to work

As a four-year-old your horse is still a year or two off maturity, but he is now strong enough to be able to undertake a moderate amount of real work allied with his further education; the word moderate is important. Too much stress during this year may not appear to do him any harm, but it could set up trouble later on; a prime cause of unsoundness in adult horses is that they were worked too hard too young. Resist the temptation to cash in on the fact that your youngster has benefited from a gradual and thorough education. It will pay dividends later on. Many events are open to four-year-olds, while others, particularly some of the stress events, are only open to five-year-olds and over. During the horse's four-year-old year, explore the avenues that are open to you and do give your horse the chance to become accustomed to working in strange company as well as that of his regular companions.

Join your local riding club. Many hold informal training sessions, some specifically for young horses. This would be of great benefit to him, not so much from the tuition aspect but to get him used to being schooled in a different place with strange horses, and as a member of a group. It does not mean you have to act upon all recommendations as to his schooling. Useful pointers will be given to you, but you may disagree with certain aspects of tuition. You should know by now what will work for your horse and what will not. Any group lesson can only give a broad outline of schooling. Remind yourself, when listening to advice, not to take everyone else's word as gospel, but also not to close your mind to what may be useful. Many people become thoroughly confused because they have been to so many instructors, none of whom agree entirely with one another. Others remain rigid and expect their horses to conform to a set of 'book rules'. Horses by no means always behave in a simple straightforward manner and any book should only be read as a good guide. It is up to the individual to apply information gained according to his own particular horse.

A common misconception, voiced even by adults, is that because a horse is the owner's pride and joy, he is raring to obey out of affection. Horses do not have this type of affection, in the way a dog has. They do, however, build up a great amount of rapport and respect if firmly and fairly treated. Some need firmer handling then others; some respond to a gentler approach; some occasionally rebel and have a stubborn tantrum and then the owner will have to be just a little bit more stubborn than the horse. Occasionally there will be an individual who is chameleon-like, with good days and bad days and great tact and clever handling will be needed with him. My own young stallion Zoltan is like this; mild as can be one day and fully co-operative, yet up to silly nonsense another. When this mood prevails indifference on my part seems to bring about a palpable sense of deflation on his and then he straightens up and gets sensible.

As well as training sessions offered by your local riding club, take part in other activities, such as pleasure rides and club shows. Do not allow your horse's inexperience to put you off. At four years of age find out as much about your horse as possible. Pleasure rides will tell you a tremendous amount about his capabilities and temperament. Do not take him on rides likely to develop into a mad scramble with undisciplined riding. If a group leader is a seasoned long distance rider, he or she will recognize the serious rider from

Right: Preparing a young horse for a show. For an impeccable turnout, it is a good idea to shampoo the mane and it is useful to have a helper to hold and reassure the horse. It is vital to accustom him to having his head handled very early in his education.

those hoping for a day's outing and will cater for the steadier riders in the group, keeping a good pace for sufficient length of time to enable both young and older horses to settle into a good rhythm. This will exercise the older horses sufficiently and be a definite help to youngsters who will have the example of the older ones to copy and get a good impression of what it means to ride in group company in open country. Avoid getting grouped with a bunch of riders who permit their mounts to dawdle along then jig when trying to catch up; or worse, have a choppy canter from rear to front to liven proceedings. These riders are a menace to both novice and seasoned horses and are behaving in a very unmannerly fashion. A good group leader should tactfully caution them and if you have got a young horse, it is a good idea to tell the leader beforehand. Distances of around 24 km (15 miles) lasting for about $2\frac{1}{2}$ to 3 hours are fine for a four-year-old and towards the end of the autumn he can quite happily cover a longer distance, provided no difficult terrain is encountered.

Many small shows have classes for novice horses and also open classes for the general type of riding horse. The most that will be required is that the horse gives a calm performance at walk, trot, canter, halt, back up, with a small individual show from each contestant. It is usual for a judge to ask for a figure eight in the individual show and this implies the movement at the canter with the choice of either a simple, or a flying, change of lead. In the simple change come down to trot for about two or three strides then pick up the opposite lead. The flying change, of which few four-year-olds are capable unless very highly schooled, is, as its name implies, done with no trot stride but a neat change of leads in the air. Any judge worth his salt will give higher marks to a good simple change than a bad flying change.

These ridden classes will be a good test for your youngster to see if your homework works away from home and also to see how well-mannered he is in company, particularly as some untoward happenings can occur if there are many entries in a smallish ring. Do not allow yourself to be boxed in, use the whole ring area to show your horse. Do not get stuck behind slower moving horses. If you do, it is quite in order to cut loose from the line or bunch and find a free space, even if you have to cross the arena to do so, or you can halt your horse for a few paces. The walk is most likely to cause a bunch up because so few horses walk on well. When you are asked to line up, follow the ring steward's orders and make sure you give your horse plenty of room. It will not be only your horse you have to watch out for, but other competitors who may be new to showing as well.

In the USA, in most novice classes the horse will not be required to perform an individual show or test. Novice classes in the USA are often referred to as 'green' or 'maiden' events. Preferably line up at an end unless the horses have been called in in a particular order. You should practise at home before the show, so your horse will stand still and calm.

Jumping

If you want to jump, start by giving your horse experience at informal club events, or small shows with 'clear round jumping' with fences at about 75 cm (2 ft 6 in) in classes where speed is not required. In the USA there are many non-recognized shows (shows not sanctioned by the American Horse Shows Association) and schooling events with 'Low Hunter' classes. Also, at some of the AHSA shows there are non-recognized classes called 'Low Hunter' or 'Baby Green', which may have very low fences. More horses are ruined by having to go against the clock before they

Trotting over poles is a useful exercise for improving the horse's balance and smoothness of pace; they must be properly spaced according to the stride of the particular horse. This will help develop the horse's suppleness, even length of stride, balance, and ability to pick up his feet.

Cubhunting usually starts in September after the
harvest, and is, traditionally, followed 'by permission of
the Master'. For a young horse it is a very useful
introduction to hunting proper, in early November.
Fields are small and there is not much galloping; the
youngster can learn to stand patiently and become
familiar with hounds, the sound of the horn, other
horses and general excitement, before he is subjected
to the more rigidly enforced discipline of foxhunting
later on.

really know what they are doing than by anything else in show jumping. At four years of age, they are very impressionable and you do not want your hard work of stabilizing his performance ruined by having to ask him to race against time. Jumping a three-year-old is just not on. The concussive effects of landing, on still-forming joints, will create more damage than the meagre rewards of a few rosettes warrant. Many showjumpers have a limited useful life because they are jumped too young. By rights, a good horse should last well into his late teens and beyond and still be sound in his limbs. He will not if those limbs are abused as a three and four-year-old. This is why any hints on jumping have been left until this chapter.

Start the youngster off with his jumping in a very progressive manner. Do not aim for any height at all, but bring him on slowly, first of all with poles on the ground, both natural and coloured; then use cavaletti at various heights. Make it very simple to start with by getting him used to trotting through a series of five or six poles spaced a stride (about 1.5 m or 4 ft 6 in) apart. This will teach him to pick his feet up and to engage his hocks. When he is going through these competently, place a cavaletto at its middle height at the end of the line of poles and he should easily trot over this. Then repeat, but with the cavaletto at its maximum height when he will need to make a small jump. All the time he is going through these exercises you should have your weight off his loins and lean very slightly forward. Your hands should have him on light contact, but as he will at first probably be a little clumsy with his first few attempts at jumping the single cavaletto, be careful not to jag him in the mouth. This will have the triple effect of making him afraid for his mouth, sending his head up out of control, and hollowing his back. Sit as still as possible in the saddle and when he reaches

the small jump, give him a squeeze with your legs to indicate takeoff.

Once he has become adept at poles and a single cavaletto, place several cavaletti in your arena and start the horse on his jumping, initially out of a trot. When he has realized there is no need for excitement – jumping nearly always elicits some excitement from even the calmest of horses – you can try the same at a canter. Try to have the horse moving very steadily forward at an easy canter and do not let him speed up before each cavaletto. Do not repeat these exercises so often that the horse gets careless, tries to speed up and treats small obstacles with contempt. Also, do not repeat the poles and cavaletti work till the animal is sick of them. Introduce small jumps about 60 cm (2 ft) high consisting of poles, low brush fences and readily available forty gallon oil drums on their sides. It is a good idea to lunge the horse over such small fences, placed in the lunging area, before riding him, as if he familiarizes himself with them this way, he will be less likely to say 'no thank you' the first time he is asked under saddle. Many horses that are chronic refusers have the seeds of such refusals sown by a too-hurried introduction to the basics of jumping. Others are pushed too fast and too high before they have fully learnt the craft and then they get scared by it.

If at all possible, use natural obstacles as well as coloured ones, as some horses are good with one, and refuse the other. You may have to arrange to go away from home for some of the jumping practice as jumps are very expensive. Unless you can provide solid obstacles your work will not be very satisfactory, as a horse will respect solidity, and very soon get to know that flimsy jumps do not hurt at all if he jumps through, rather than over them. Jumping away from home has the added advantage of teaching the horse to jump anywhere; some are paragons

An early jumping lesson – a solid, low fence,
encouraging the young horse to perform well, as is
indicated by his keen, calm attitude and good
clearance.

at home and stick their toes in at shows.

Once the jumps can be raised from over
the 60 cm (2 ft) height start bringing a little
breadth into them, as later on, if you intend
doing much jumping, your horse will have to
jump spreads. He will also have to jump
combinations, with one, two, or three strides
between fences. All these aspects can be
taught with low fences and if he is not rushed,
or jumped to excess, he will later be able to
go up the scale till he is really proficient and
athletic and enjoys his jumping.

Vary the jumps as much as possible, both in location and type. Once the horse has learnt the simplest methods of jumping on a continuous track around the arena, place jumps in the middle at angles so that he has to learn to turn while still maintaining stride and impulsion. Later on, when he is very confident, he should be taught to jump obstacles where perhaps the striding is not perfect. He is going to meet this someday so he had better learn at home. When getting a horse ready for jumping, it is a good idea to have someone else join you for practice sessions; and to watch for faults that need correcting. Schooling on the flat seems best done in solitude, but jumping, because of its competitive nature, is more satisfactory done in company.

Even if you intend using your young horse primarily as a showjumper eventually, his four-year-old year is not the time to concentrate on this. Give him just enough to keep him interested, and little enough to make sure he will stay sound for the many years when you may be jumping him a lot.

Around early September hounds are out cubbing and as the meets are early in the morning and the fields not enormous, take your youngster cubhunting occasionally. Hunting excites most horses so it is much better for a youngster to start when the pace is likely to be slow and there are few riders.

He can learn to accept hounds milling around him, on occasions even passing between his legs. If he had to put up with this for the first time at a regular meet, with a lot of horses present, the whole atmosphere of excited horses, plus hounds might be too much for him and he could commit the inexcusable crime of kicking a hound, or even stepping on one. A few early risings on your part will give him the opportunity to get used to the hunting scene. Young hounds will be out for the first few times as well, and without the crush of horses, should there prove to be a moderate run, your own youngster will not get as excited as he would with a whole field thundering along. Cubbing tends to be more leisurely as it is a teaching session for hounds. Provided your young horse is normally very well-mannered, it can prove a very good teaching ground for him. If possible take along an impeccably-mannered stable companion for him to copy.

At the end of your horse's four-year-old year you should have a very good idea of what he is best suited for. You will have seen what he is good at and enjoys; what he dislikes; and what he just tolerates. If you have shown him, you will have an idea if he is the type the judges like and if he has that certain 'presence' required of a show-horse. Some actively dislike shows, doing far better at 'real work'.

9

Basic health

Only fairly common health hazards and those particularly found in youngsters, are dealt with here. Most can be averted by the use of preventative medicine.

Internal parasites

All horses are subject to worms and should be treated regularly to keep the worm burden down. A dose every six to eight weeks is necessary unless the horse is on very well managed pasture, preferably grazed jointly with cattle. Your vet will advise as to the best product to use; remember that not all anthelmintics destroy all worms; those that do are not necessarily equally effective against all varieties. Study the small print to see what each preparation deals with.

In addition to the normal range of worms such as ascarids, strongyles, and occasionally tapeworm the horse can also be affected by bots and lungworm.

Bots

Worm for bots at least once a year; the best time is in early winter after the first hard frost. By then the bot flies have died, no more eggs will be laid and the horse will have come into his winter coat which will be free of bot eggs. With a quiet horse, the eggs may be removed carefully from the coat using a blunt blade in a safety razor.

The bot fly lays its yellow eggs in late summer and autumn on the horse's forelegs, chest, front of shoulders and mane near the withers. He ingests the eggs when scratching with his teeth, they hatch to larvae and penetrate the mucous membrane in the tongue, lips and gums. The larvae travel to the stomach and attach to the lining where they cause much damage. The larvae feed and mature until spring when they are expelled, bright red, in dung, to hatch out and re-start the cycle.

Lungworm

Lungworm is not as common in horses. It is frequently caused by having a horse turned out with an infected donkey. The donkey may appear perfectly healthy but still be a host and if the horse starts coughing it would be wise to have samples of faeces of both horse and donkey analysed. Grass will be contaminated so it would be wise to keep horses off that field for six months. Lungworm is extremely rare, if not non-existent, in horses in the USA.

Colic

There are several varieties and several causes of this. A massive infestation of worms may cause a horse to get colic, particularly a youngster who is more susceptible. Other causes are: a heavy feed after excessive work; working on a full stomach; mouldy feeds; icy cold water being drunk by a very hot horse; general debility followed by a sudden change to high nutrition. Some horses which are well fed will also colic after a sudden diet change, if their stomachs are sensitive. Symptoms of colic are: general unease; breaking out into a sweat; repeated looking back at the flank; kicking at the stomach. Some horses with colic get down and try rolling to alleviate the pain. This should be prevented or a fatal twisted gut could result; walking around, while not stopping the attack, will prevent the animal lying down.

Good management is the obvious answer, certainly your youngster should never have got to the stage of having a heavy worm burden. If the colic is for any of the other reasons and it is of a mild nature, give him a warm sloppy bran mash and keep a watch on him. If it does not decrease within about an hour call the vet. If it is severe call the vet immediately. Most colics are avoidable by using common sense in the first place.

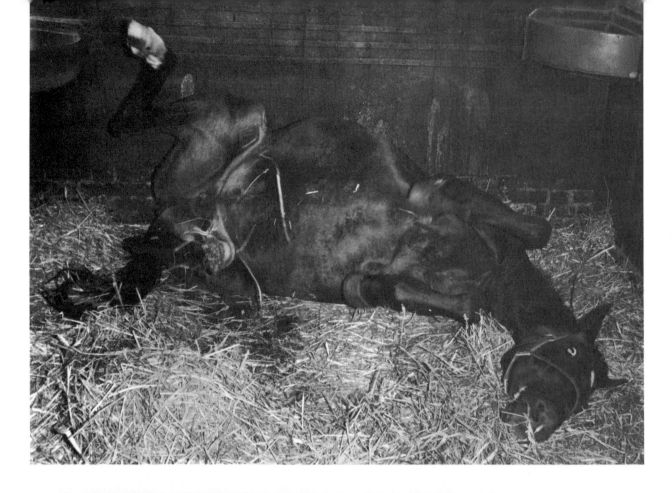

Tetanus

This is fairly rare nowadays because almost all horses are injected against it as foals with boosters given as required. Do not think that when the horse has his final shot of the series he is protected for life. It used erroneously to be called 'life immunization'; its effect lasts only about three years, after which another booster should be given. If the horse should contract tetanus its symptoms will be a rigidity in the whole body with head and tail extended. The horse will have great difficulty in moving. The head will be unable to be lowered, or moved laterally. Mastication will be difficult and maybe impossible. Severe cases rarely recover; those that do are immune for life. Puncture wounds are the normal cause.

Influenza

There has been a great surge of this menace in the last few years and when 'the cough' breaks out in a district it travels like wildfire. The horse will be generally run down, coughing badly, especially after exertion and there will be a discharge from the nostrils accompanied by a high temperature. The best course is prevention by injection each year. The first year he will have two at monthly intervals, thereafter a yearly booster. During an attack all work must stop and the horse be isolated, as influenza is highly contagious. The injections for tetanus and influenza can be given in a joint vaccine.

Above left: Signs of colic include rolling and lying on the back. The belly is distended by gases formed inside.

Below left: A pony suffering from strangles. The enlarged gland (submandibular) between the jaws is being demonstrated.

Right: Making a hypodermic injection into the muscles of the hindquarters.

Strangles

This is a disease occasioned by a streptococcus virus and attacks the lymph glands of the head. Affected horses will have a large hard lump form under the jaw, which will enlarge and become softer before breaking. There will also be a purulent yellowish discharge from the nostrils. The horse may be off his feed, most certainly in a severe attack, and in any case will have difficulty chewing and swallowing, due to the swelling under his jaw. It is extremely contagious both at the stage of discharge from the nostrils and when the abscess bursts. It occurs mostly in young horses and though debilitating, is rarely fatal if the animal was previously in good health. Having had it, the animal gains a certain, but not total, immunity from the disease. Older horses may contract strangles but it is less likely after the age of six. Another form of the disease is known as bastard strangles, where the disease attacks internally. It is much rarer, but also more dangerous and often fatal. Affected animals should be isolated and anything in contact with them

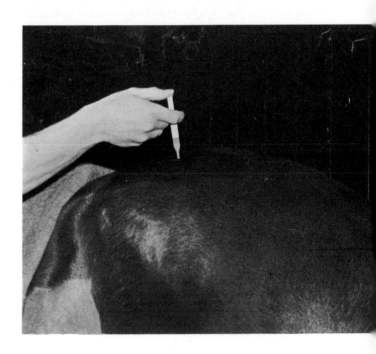

be disinfected or burnt. The illness usually runs its course in about six weeks, when the horse should no longer be able to pass the infection on.

Splints

These are one of the commonest causes of temporary lameness in young horses and occur when the splint bone sustains a fracture; when the ligament that attaches the splint bone to the cannon bone becomes inflamed; or when the outer lining of the bone becomes inflamed. At first the horse may appear lame only spasmodically, particularly on hard going, but when the lameness recurs without any apparent cause, it is wise to suspect splints. The most common sites of splints are the insides of the forelimb cannon bones, although they can occur on the outside and on the hind legs. Most are caused by concussion, but may also be caused by the inside of the cannon bone being struck by the opposite hoof. There will usually be heat at the site of the splint and there may be a hard lump varying in size from barely discernible to one that is quite prominent and very hard. Rest for a period of about six weeks is usually enough for the aggravation to cease, but the enlargement may remain. If it is only a fibrous tissue enlargement, this will eventually regress. If actual bone is being laid down as the result of a blow, it will result in a permanent lump which, if not too large, can be diminished by faithful applications of Workalin over a period of months. In the USA, your veterinarian may advise one of two approaches to treating splints; either reducing them or treating with irritants. Azium, usually mixed with DMSO as a penetrating agent, has a reducing effect. Provided splints do not interfere with action, or the suspensory ligaments and the tendons, there is no cause for alarm, as the lameness will subside. If it does not, an X-ray will determine its exact cause and the necessary treatment other than rest.

Laminitis

This is another cause of very bad lameness in horses and is caused by inflammation of the laminae of the hoof. It causes the horse great pain and the affected hooves will be very hot. If you can imagine pain caused by an abscess under a nail, you can appreciate what inflammation under an unexpandible horny hoof will feel like.

Laminitis, sometimes called 'founder' in the USA, can be brought on by various causes; the most common being too rich feeding, especially too rich grass; it can also be caused by allowing a very hot and exhausted horse to swill ice cold water after great exertion, thus interfering with the normal cooling down process of the blood. Horses that carry an excess of flesh, or are overtopped, are more prone to it than the lighter framed types.

Veterinary attention should be obtained as there are modern drugs that can help. Other treatments are a cut back to a poor diet; restriction of lush grazing; standing the horse in cold running water; or placing the hooves in sacking lined with plastic in which crushed ice has been placed. In a severe case dropped soles may result. Laminitis can and should be prevented by good management.

10

Basic feeding

All horses require plenty of good quality feedstuffs, clean water, adequate stabling, and good grazing.

Grass keep

For most horse owners, particularly those operating on a limited area of land, the grass keep will need to be supplemented by grain and hay. In the height of summer grass may be of sufficient quality and quantity to provide all the nourishment needed, provided the horse is not working. However, many pastures which are not fertilized and cared for are almost empty of nutritional value even at the height of their season, especially in the more arid US regions. For about eight months of the year there is always the need for additional feed. In winter the horse will rely completely on being fed by you, as the grass will stop growing and what is left will have very little nutritional value.

The feeding of the pregnant mare was dealt with in Chapter 3. As most foals are born in early to mid-spring, pasture maintenance for grazing purposes is discussed first.

It usually takes a minimum of 4050 sq m (one acre) of good grazing to furnish feed for one horse. Very little of the acreage on which most horses live is top quality grazing, unless it belongs to a large stud, or is part of a farm where cattle are kept. Land these days is too expensive to give the best to non-productive horses. If you own the land, the maintenance is completely in your hands and you can manage it better than if it is shared.

Horses are fussy feeders, eating only the best short sweet grass, avoiding any which has been dung fouled. Therefore grass in these areas grows long and is soured, as well as being a host for parasites which infest dung and migrate on to clean grass. A good way to get the most from your pasture is to pick up the dung regularly. This will make more of the paddock available for grazing and lessen the parasite infestation and horses will thrive better. Alternatively, if there is sufficient grazing it is a good idea to run some calves in with the horses. They will eat the longer grasses that horses leave and in so doing, ingest the migrating parasites from the horse dung. They will not harm the calves, and parasites from calves will not harm horses.

Much grazing is lost by the land carrying a very high proportion of weeds. If your pasture is weed ridden, either spray it early enough in the season to kill the weeds, or be prepared to lay it up for a sufficient time later. If you spray in spring or summer it will have to be left for a few weeks (according to manufacturers' instructions) before you can turn animals back on to it. In the USA weeds such as thistle, ragweed, larkspur and loco weed ruin pastures. The last two are poisonous. Other weeds occur in different regions. The most common weeds in Britain which ruin pasture are thistles, docks, buttercups, and ragwort. The last two are poisonous, buttercups only mildly so, but ragwort, if eaten in quantity, is lethal. Ragwort is rarely eaten in the green stage because nature warns animals by the foul smell, but dry, it loses its smell but retains the poison; so be very careful when buying hay to make sure it is made from fields that are free from this weed. Ragwort is also one of the noxious weeds that the law requires to be removed. The only way really to get rid of it is to pull it methodically each year when it flowers and gradually the problem is brought under control. It is worth knowing that if there is a field close by riddled with ragwort and the owner does nothing about it and the seeds are replanting your ragwort-free paddock, you can, if all else fails, apply to your council to have them enforce the weeds' removal. Thistles are also best pulled up by the roots and once cleared, do not come back.* Horses relish wilted thistles. Nettles thrive, particularly in dung-infested areas. If the field is ragwort free, a mid-summer topping of all unwanted weeds is a help in keeping them under control. If ragwort is present, clear it before topping. Sour land benefits from a dressing of chalk and depleted soils can be top dressed with nitrogen at about 100 kg to 4050 sq m (2 cwt to the acre). Naturally this must be done out of the grazing season – preferably late in the year in order to give spring growth a chance.

Hays

Unfortunately, although superb hay can be made in Britain this is very much at the mercy of the weather. Unless money is no object, quite often buying hay does not always mean buying the best quality, which may be prohibitive in price. However, the main things to look for are: hay that has been harvested before it went to seed; hay that has not been rained on; or baled before it has dried sufficiently; hay that has been made from a weed-free field. Buy from a reputable source and if possible go and see it before buying. It should have a pleasant fragrance with no hint of mustiness. There are several varieties of hay, soft meadow hay, the harder timothies, and best of all but very scarce alfalfa (lucerne). Poor quality hay has a very low protein content and the best, apart from alfalfa, only about 7 to 10 per cent at most. Alfalfa can have almost double that amount, and should be fed with care as some horses do too well on it and get digestive problems. It is more expensive. Horses mostly do best on the harder hays, but alfalfa is excellent.

* In parts of the USA the thistle is illegal and must be removed.

Protein

Most feeds can be broken down into starch content and protein content; the latter term in often very misleading. When a feed is quoted as having, say, 13 per cent protein, it does not mean that the horse is actually getting that in his diet; the Total Digestible Nutrient from the 13 per cent is approximately half that figure. Therefore it is important to choose the best qualities of feed with the higher protein content. In fact if a mature horse did get the quoted protein amount from his feeds he would be getting too much. Humans thrive on very high protein foods for energy, but a horse needs those which are high in starch; so when feeding a horse the basic guide should be to feed high quality, high protein; when in hard work, feeds with a high starch content.

Sweetfeed

In the USA commercially prepared mixes that include oats and corn are very popular feeds.

Grains

Oats
Oats are usually weighed at so many pounds to the bushel (weight per volume), and the heavier the oat the better the quality – more kernel, less husk. They can be fed whole, crushed, bruised or crimped. Whole oats sometimes pass straight through the digestive system, crushed can lose a portion of their value in heavy crushing and need to have a binding agent to stop the horse fluffing some of the nutrient out of his feed tub. Bruised are best as they are more easily digestible and lose little in the bruising process. Protein content of oats is between 11 and 13 per cent depending on quality. Bad oats contain considerably less.

Barley

Barley used not to be fed to horses in quantity, but nowadays it is recognized as being a good feed, almost as high in protein as oats, with a higher starch equivalent. Therefore, weight for weight one can feed less. If fed whole it should be soaked and cooked; raw it should be cracked or crushed. I have fed barley in quantity for years and have never had any stomach upsets or cases of impaction. However, if you introduce it into a horse's diet, do it gradually, particularly if his stomach is not cast iron.

Maize or corn

This is similar in starch content to barley but slightly lower in protein. It is a good fattening feed but should be given sparingly. In Britain it is always fed flaked, but in the USA it is fed whole or on the cob. It is considerably harder than the barley kernel.

Beetpulp

This is useful for winter feeding, adding bulk and variety; it is good for fleshing a horse out. It should not be fed in quantity at any one time and should be well soaked beforehand. When a horse is not working much he can be fed more – 0.9–1.4 kg (2–3 lb) dry weight a day, but in hard work it should be eliminated from his diet, except for a handful to moisten his feed.

Bran

These days feeding bran is really too expensive, except in occasional mashes, for the good it does. It is a traditional food, but if fed in great quantities with oats it nullifies a lot of the oats' goodness, oats being relatively low in calcium while bran is very high in phosphorus. Very little should be fed to avoid mineral imbalance.

Salts

Iodized salt should either be readily available in the form of a lick or be added frequently to the feed at the rate of approximately 25 g (1 oz) per day and more if the weather is very hot and the horse's work very demanding. Mineral salt licks are also good, as they offer trace minerals plus salt. Some horses will not use their licks and also sift loose salt from their feed. Although normal feeds contain certain natural salts, additional salt is needed. If the horse refuses it or sifts it out, liquify a crushed block and add a little salty water to his feed once or twice a week, or soak the beetpulp in salted water.

Vitamin and mineral supplements

These are absolutely legion so ask your vet's advice, which should be impartial. However, if a good diet is maintained and the horse is healthy, supplements should not be necessary.

Feeding for growth

Grazing is at its best in May, June and July, when the protein content of grass is at its highest. Thereafter, it loses quality until by the end of September growth has slowed down and it will probably be necessary to start supplementing with hay and grain, unless you have unlimited acreage.

A young foal can be fed a small amount of grain as soon as he can be got on to it. When with his dam, feed about 0.45 kg (1 lb) a day, either in her feed tub if she permits it, or in a creep feeder (see page 49) if she is greedy and selfish with him. This will suffice while she is lactating and giving him all he needs, provided grazing is ample. Towards the fifth and sixth month, and just before weaning, it is a good idea to increase his hard feed to two small feeds a day so that he is getting between

1.4–1.8 kg (3–4 lb) a day for himself in total. By this time the grass will be slowing in growth, so he will also be used to sharing the hay ration. At weaning time, provided he has been eating adult food, the adjustment in his diet from milk to hard feed and hay will not be too difficult. When you wean him he will need to be kept in for a day or so and provided he relishes his rations he should not lose too much condition.

It usually takes about a week for a six-month-old foal to get on to his full ration. A foal which is expected to mature at approximately 15.2 hands and 453 kg (1,000 lb) in weight should get about 3.6 kg (8 lb) hard feed a day with unlimited hay. A close watch should be kept on his condition and as his size increases towards yearling stage, his rations will be gradually increased till he is eating about 4.5 kg (10 lb) a day. To make the feed more palatable add about 0.9 kg (2 lb) a day dry weight of beetpulp. This should be well soaked overnight and will triple its bulk when wet. If fed dry, you risk an acute case of colic or impaction when the swelling takes place inside the stomach. Any hay should be top quality; foals and youngsters do not at first eat as much as older horses so it is wasteful and denying them the good start they need, to feed poor quality.

Remember that after a foal starts on full feed, he should be fed as if he is a horse, not a foal. The first year of his life is the most important nutritionally as he reaches more than half his final body weight in that time. As a yearling, two and three-year-old he is still growing and care should be taken to feed him enough, bearing in mind when using a feed chart that growing equates with work (see chart on page 31). As a guide, feed the yearling to two-year-old 0.56 kg (1.25 lb) per 45 kg (100 lb) of body weight and as a two to three-year-old reduce it to 0.45 kg (1 lb) per 45 kg (100 lb) of body weight.

When the youngster is in any form of training or schooling the ration should be stepped up to the next bracket because he cannot grow and work on the lower rung of the ration scale. It is a mistake to think that keeping him short during breaking will make him more docile. If it does you will only have to do the job again properly later on and it could put a lot of stress on him.

No chart answers all feeding problems. Watch your youngster's condition. You want him to thrive, but you do not want him gross and overtopped for limbs as yet undeveloped. Keep an eye on progress and development. Some need less feed, some more, according to their metabolism. All youngsters go through the ugly duckling stage of appearing out of proportion. Their limbs are gangly, hindquarters higher than the withers, neck still a little straight, and often ribs show. This will be most noticeable at about the yearling stage and will last a few months. Weanlings well over the separation stage look all of a piece, then through the next twelve months, they seem to fill out, get lean, then fill out again, and in a matter of weeks can put on a lot. Naturally no youngster can grow up and out at the same time, so apparent lean stages should not unduly worry you when the youngster has a clear eye, glossy coat, and is full of life. If he gets a dull coat, loses vigour and gets pot-bellied, suspect a heavy worm burden. Young horses up to two years old are far more susceptible to this than older horses (see pages 49 and 109). Worm him regularly, even at three week intervals if necessary.

When he is a four-year-old in normal work he should be fed just like any other horse, with a ration of about 0.45 kg (1 lb) per 45 kg (100 lb) body weight. When in a rest period, cut it back slightly. As a five-year-old the rations should be commensurate with whatever work he is going to do and for some it could well mean the top level of feeding.

11

Five years old: future prospects

Over the past five years you have watched your young horse grow into a mature animal and have educated him to be ready to take part in the wide spectrum open to a five-year-old. As a four-year-old, he will have been out and about, observing and learning some of the things his adult life will have to offer; now he is ready to begin taking an active part. A few of the less strenuous events will have been open to four-year-olds, but, and rightly so, most associations do not permit a horse younger than five to take part in their full range of activities. Here is a brief summary of the activities likely to appeal to most riders, and within the scope of most horses' capabilities. Cost is an important factor in deciding what activities to undertake;

Versatile mare at a nice trot, ridden with a very light hand and relaxing to the Walking Horse bit.

when costing bear annual inflation in mind. Addresses of associations and societies are listed at the end of the book. Consider joining the ones relevant to your interests. Associations will have a yearly subscription which will be indicated on forms sent to those requesting information. Many societies require all competitors in their activities to be members, others do not, but charge non-members a higher fee. Addresses of societies not listed are obtainable from the British Horse Society, or the American Horse Council in the USA.

Pleasure riding

Most young horses, by the time they are five will have received sufficient schooling to enable them to give their owners a very pleasurable ride. Many riders keep horses mainly for the sheer fun and companionship they offer without wanting to be competitive. However, if you would like to try entering for a show class it is the simplest, and least costly, of all equestrian activities. Here are some things your young horse should be able to do.

If he is shown under English tack he will be able to take part in such classes as 'Family Horse' or 'Pony', 'Riding Horse Class', and if he is a pedigree and registered animal, in the various ridden classes run by Breed Societies. For these, he will be expected to perform at walk, trot and canter on both reins; maybe do a hand gallop, halt quietly and back up without resistance. He must also accept another rider and perform willingly for him or her, as in Britain judges frequently ride the horses they are judging. Most judges ask for an individual show, sometimes leaving

Left: The same six-year-old mare going at an extremely well balanced canter. Note the loose rein and Walking Horse bit. The mare's head position is good; she is flexing well at the poll. The rider wears a Western hat, shirt, boots and leather chaps – correct turnout for Western pleasure riding. The roping saddle has a rear (cinch) girth to help take the strain put on the saddle horn. The bridle has split reins and a 20 cm (8 in) shank to the curb bit, the severity of which is governed by the curb strap tension. Note the mare's closed mouth and the happy expression on her face.

Below: The same mare going equally kindly in a Pelham bit and English tack, at trot.

it to the individuals, sometimes asking for certain movements to be included in the show. In the USA it is rare for a pleasure horse to be asked to perform an individual test. The horse will not be ridden by anyone other than the owner.

If you choose to show your horse under Western tack, he will be able to be shown in 'Western Pleasure', 'Western Riding' and 'Trail' Classes; if he goes well both English and Western, in the 'Versatility' Class. For a 'Pleasure Class' he must walk, jog, lope on both reins and back up. In 'Western Riding', 'Reining', 'Stock' and 'Medal' classes he is expected to be able to do a figure eight showing lead changes and a halt.

In 'Western Riding' he will be expected to negotiate a simple pattern mostly at lope showing flying changes of lead in each direction, as well as incorporating opening and closing a gate, walking, jogging, halting and backing up. In 'Trail' he may negotiate a variety of obstacles; backing up incorporating a ninety degree turn, his rider putting on and taking off a slicker (raincoat), loading into a trailer, crossing a wooden bridge, leading another horse, a small jump, leading over a jump, dragging a heavy log, ground tying (standing still when the reins hang down); and he must give a comfortable and mannerly ride. In 'Versatility' he will be expected to go under both English and Western saddles and show the differences in the gaits for each style.

For Western riding, the horse has slower and more relaxed gaits at jog and lope and he must go on a loose rein and also neck rein. This is one of the reasons why it is useful to teach the horse to go freely on light contact and to understand the uses of the indirect rein (also known as neck-reining). For a horse well-schooled in English riding, teaching him to go Western should not be difficult, and can be very rewarding.

Endurance riding

If you have taken part in group activities, with your horse as a four-year-old, particularly pleasure rides, you will now have a good notion of how your mount reacts to being in company and also whether he is stimulated enough really to give of himself on a ride. If he comes alive when on a ride and is always ready for a few extra kilometres (miles), rather than thinking of cutting for home, and his stride is very fluid, and not tiring, yet capable of real drive, then long distance riding could be his forte.

In Britain there are three societies that cater for the long distance enthusiast and these are:

Endurance Horse and Pony Society, a national body dealing solely with promoting the interests of long distance riders and horses. Rides are 40 to 160 km (25–100 miles).

The Arab Horse Society which is keen to promote the Arabian as a long distance horse. It holds several rides a year, from the pleasure ride to their yearly Marathon.

The British Horse Society which has a section devoted to the sport. It runs rides from 32 to 160 km (20 to 100 miles) in one day, with some major rides 160 km (100 miles) run over more than one day.

As a guide to US Long Distance Riding, *see* Useful addresses.

The minimum age for most rides in the above groups is five, with the exception of the EHPS which permits four-year-olds in Competitive Trail Riding at the lowest grade of Novice Horse and at a distance not in excess of 40 km (25 miles) and at speeds of 10–11.25 km (6 to 7 miles) per hour.

A veterinary inspection on a long distance ride. These are carried out before the ride, at compulsory halts and spot check points, and at the finish. Veterinary supervision helps to prevent horses being over-ridden.

An endurance horse can certainly be used for most other activities, but it is rare to find the true endurance horse being shown, as due to the distances and the speeds required in the higher grades of the sport, he will be fit and not carrying the spare fat, which unfortunately show judges seem to want. As in this chapter we have come full circle with the youngster, it is worth mentioning that any mare or stallion that has achieved consistent success in endurance riding would be a very good animal to breed from, as he or she will be sound, proven under stress, and most probably be very stable in temperament – three essentials for a successful long distance horse.

Preparing a horse for a full season of long distance is going to cost considerably more in feed than a horse in light work, and his shoeing bill will be high, as most rules require a horse to be adequately shod, and this in real terms means freshly shod. Entry fees vary according to the length of the ride. However, the value for money from these entry fees is considerably more than for a brief go round a jumping course, or for the half hour spent in a show class. Each horse has at least two thorough vettings before and after the competition, first to determine his competence to start; after the ride, his condition measured against that of other competitors. To get any award at all, the horse must pass his final vetting in a 'condition fit to proceed', should it be required.

On longer distance rides, additional vettings are performed and a great deal of knowledge can be gained about one's own and other people's horses under stress.

The season for long distance starts in March and goes on till October. The EHPS holds approximately twelve competitive events during this time and the BHS, a series of 64 km (40 mile) qualifiers, plus their major events, the most prestigious being the Golden Horseshoe. The EHPS has an accumulative points system and awards at the end of the year. BHS rules require all riders to be aged 17 or over and horses to be a minimum of 14 hands. EHPS has an adult section of 18 and over and a junior section of 10 through 17 years. There is no restriction on height of animal, provided that in the veterinarian judges' opinion the horse or pony is up to the weight it is expected to carry.

Hunting

Hunting is carried on in regions of widely varied terrain, mostly with foxhounds, sometimes with harriers or buckhounds. In the western USA some hunts chase coyote. Any size of horse or pony is suitable, but naturally the type of going will influence the type of horse that is best for the job. In heavily wooded areas, a tall rangy horse is a definite disadvantage owing to the amount of time spent avoiding trees. In heavy going, a horse with a good bit of substance is needed. In areas such as moorland, where ground can be treacherous, a handy horse with a fair bit of native 'savvy' regarding bogs is an asset.

The costs of hunting are considerable. Subscriptions vary with different hunts. There will also be Field Money. There is usually a higher subscription if you wish to hunt more than one day a week, or with some packs if you wish to hunt more than one horse. Feeding and shoeing costs will be higher for hunting than for ordinary hacking. There will be transport costs, unless you hunt only when the meet is local. If you hunt only occasionally, you would normally only be permitted three days hunting per pack, before being expected to become a full member.

The hunting season starts with cubbing in early September. The opening meet is usually

the first Saturday in November and hunting finishes with most packs at the end of March. A hunt's activities are governed by the farmers' sowing and harvesting seasons.

If you intend hunting, your horse must be well-mannered in company and remain well-mannered even when the excitement of a good run has stirred things up. He should be able to stay behind and not be fidgety at covert side. He should also be able to cope with moderate size fences, but should he refuse, you must then go to the back of the

Quarterhorse stallion at an extended trot. His head is somewhat high. This very versatile stallion is a big winner when shown in-hand, and under saddle in dressage, jumping and Western classes.

queue and wait your turn again. Above all, he must keep his heels to himself, even in a crush of which there are plenty when moving from covert to covert, or in a confined space such as woodland tracks. When hounds are passing you should turn your horse inwards to the track, not expose his heels to hounds.

Show jumping

Show jumping can be very expensive. Unlike the events previously detailed which can be done at several levels, to get anywhere with show jumping, beyond a local show level, it is necessary to compete regularly. There is a world of difference between training at home, even over a full range of showjumps, and actually competing in the ring. In the ring, there is a definite atmosphere, which will communicate itself to the horse. Some jump all the better for it, others take quite a few shows, or a season or two, to come into their own. There are shows affiliated to the British Show Jumping Association and non-affiliated ones. In the USA there are shows affiliated with the American Horse Shows Association and others that are not (the non-affiliated are called 'non-recognized'). A showjumper may compete at any show although non-recognized shows are usually just schooling

The same Quarterhorse stallion – a successful showjumper, here he shows power and style over a practice jump at a show. His forelegs are neatly tucked in, he has stood well back and clears this jump with a lot to spare.

events. If you really want to reach a high level you must join and register your horse yearly with the BSJA. The present cost of this is about £53 per annum, but if the horse is really successful and goes through the grades it will cost correspondingly more. Registering your horse with the BSJA will preclude your jumping him at any unaffiliated show which offers more than a £7 first prize in the class you enter. There are three official grades – 'C', 'B' and 'A' for registered horses. To enter in Grade 'C' the horse must not have won more than £800 at affiliated shows; there are three sections: *Wing Newcomers*, open to horses with a total of not more than £300 prize money; *Foxhunter* with a total of not more than £500, and *Grade 'C'* as mentioned above. Show-jumpers competing in AHSA recognized shows are also classified by their earning. A Pre-liminary horse must have won less than $2500 in jumper classes or be still in his first year of showing in AHSA jumper classes; an Inter-mediate horse must have won less than $5000; any horse may compete in the Open Division. These are accumulative, not yearly, earnings.

Entry fees at small local shows are constantly changing but start at about £2.50 with a first prize of £15, and at affiliated shows from £3.50 to £5 for the Newcomer and Foxhunter classes. Prize money can be as low as £8 for a first, on up to £25 in Foxhunter classes. Naturally, the higher grade classes carry a higher entry fee. Entry numbers in most show jumping classes are very high, so the odds are not in favour of coming out financially ahead. If you enter unaffiliated classes and are a member of the BSJA, which limits the classes you may enter, it is difficult to recoup the cost of entry and travel. To give your horse a really good grounding in the sport, he will need to enter quite a few shows a year; if your ambitions range above local shows you will progress further which will be costly.

Hunter trials and driving

Hunter trials are usually held in the early spring before most shows get under way, or late autumn at the tail end of the show season. They are less formal than show jumping classes and many horses do much better over the natural obstacles, with a good bit of galloping between. They are run against the clock, the horse with the fastest time and no penalties being the winner. They are well within the scope of the average horse who is not capable of serious show jumping.

For some horses, attaining a level of proficiency in all the activities described will not be too much, although not necessarily at the top level. There are many horses and ponies which hunt in winter, give honest pleasure throughout the summer, take in a few shows entering ridden and jumping classes and some long distance rides.

Great pleasure can be derived from learn-ing to drive and training your horse to go in harness; although a vehicle and equipment will be expensive. Many horses can learn to go equally well under saddle and in harness; suitable breeds for the novice include all Welsh sections, most other native breeds and cross-breeds; the Morgan and Appaloosa; for the experienced, the Standardbred and Saddlebred, amongst others. In the USA Arabians are popular for use in harness. Horses with a great deal of Thoroughbred blood are temperamentally less suitable for driving.

It will be a long wait, watching your youngster grow to maturity. Temptations may have been strong to overdo things in his earlier years, but with patience, bringing him on slowly and teaching him thoroughly, you will find that the six year plan has been worth the effort. Your young horse will have come full circle from foal to five-year-old, ready to take over from your good mare who produced him, to continue the line.

Foals enjoy each other's company and playing provides
exercise for growth and muscle development. Except
with native ponies, it is best not to turn them out in
fields where there are steep slopes as they could damage
limbs racing up and down. It is not safe to leave a
foaling slip on in the field as the foal could catch his leg
in it while playing or scratching.

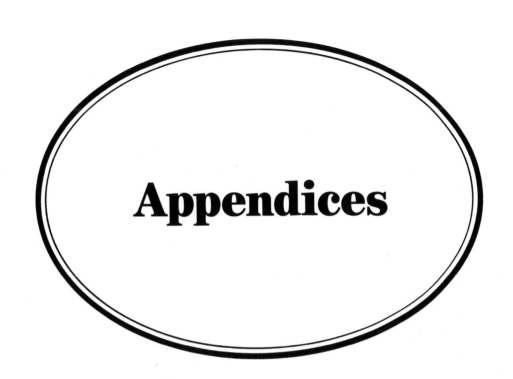

Appendices

Further reading

Available in Britain

The amateur horse breeder A.C. Leighton Hardman, PELHAM BOOKS.

Stud management Henry Wymnalen, J.A. ALLEN & CO.

Educating horses from birth to riding Peter A. Jones, ROBERT HALE.

The horse: from conception to maturity Peter Rossdale, J.A. ALLEN & CO.

Mares, foals and foaling Friedrich Andrist, J.A. ALLEN & CO.

The gentle art of horsebreaking Robbie Murray, ROBERT HALE.

Training the young horse THE PONY CLUB.

The early training of the horse R.L.V. ffrench-Blake, SEELEY SERVICE & CO.

Training the young horse, the first two years Anthony Crossley, STANLEY PAUL.

Training your own horse Mary Rose, THRESHOLD BOOKS.

The mind of your horse R.H. Smythe, J.A. ALLEN & Co.

Bily's Hunting Directory J.A. ALLEN & CO.

The Endurance Horse Ann Hyland, J.A. ALLEN

Riding Long Distance Ann Hyland, J.A. ALLEN

The Appaloosa Ann Hyland, J.A. ALLEN

The Quarter Horse Ann Hyland, J.A. ALLEN

Available in the USA

Horse nutrition, a practical guide Harold F. Hintz, PRENTICE HALL PRESS

A horse of your own M.A. Stoneridge, DOUBLEDAY

The horse's mind Lucy Rees, PRENTICE HALL PRESS

The lungeing book Judy Richter, PRENTICE HALL PRESS

Veterinary notes for horse owners Capt. M. Horace Hayes, PRENTICE HALL PRESS

The whole horse catalog S.D. Price, SIMON & SCHUSTER

Horse nutrition, a practical guide Harold F. Hintz, PRENTICE HALL PRESS

A horse of your own M.A. Stoneridge, DOUBLEDAY

The horse's mind Lucy Rees, PRENTICE HALL PRESS

The lungeing book Judy Richter, PRENTICE HALL PRESS

Veterinary notes for horse owners Capt,. M. Horace Hayes, PRENTICE HALL PRESS

The whole horse catalog S.D. Price, SIMON & SCHUSTER

Useful addresses

Britain

British Horse Society and *The Pony Club* British Equestrian Centre, Stoneleigh, Kenilworth, Warwickshire CV8 2LR

Hunters Improvement and National Light Horse Breeding Society 96 High Street, Edenbridge, Kent TN8 5AR

Thoroughbred Breeders' Association Stanstead House, The Avenue, Newmarket, Suffolk, CB8 9AA

Irish Horse Board The Irish Farm Centre (3rd Floor), Bluebell, Dublin 12, Ireland

National Foaling Bank Meretown Stud, Newport, Shropshire

British Warmblood Society Moorlands Farm, New Yatt, Witney, Oxfordshire

National Pony Society Brook House, 25 High Street, Alton, Hants GU34 1AW

Ponies Association of UK Chesham House, Green End Road, Sawtry, Huntingdon, Cambs PE17 5UY

Arab Horse Society Windsor House. Ramsbury, Marlborough, Wiltshire, SW8 2PE

Cleveland Bay Horse Society York Livestock Centre, Murton, York YO1 3UF

Irish Draught Horse Society of Great Britain 4th Street, National Agricultural Centre, Stoneleigh, Warwickshire

British Palomino Society Penrhiwllan, Llandysul, Dyfed SA44 5NZ

British Quarter Horse Association Ltd 4th Street, National Agricultural Centre, Stoneleigh, Kenilworth, Warwicks CV8 2LG

British Appaloosa Society c/o 2 Fredrick Street, Rugby, Warwicks, CV21 2EN.

British Morgan Horse Society George and Dragon Hall, Mary Place, London W11

Welsh Pony and Cob Society 6 Chalybeate Street, Aberystwyth, Dyfed SY23 1HS

Highland Pony Society Beechwood, Elie, Fife KY1 9DH

English Connemara Pony Society 2 The Leys, Salford, Chipping Norton, Oxon OX7 5FD

Connemara Pony Breeders Society 73 Dalysfort Road, Salthill, Galway, Ireland

New Forest Pony and Cattle Breeding Society Beacon Corner, Burley, Ringwood, Hants BH24 4EH

Dales Pony Society 196 Springvale Road, Walkley, Sheffield S6 3NU

Fell Pony Society 19 Dragley Beck, Ulverston, Cumbria LA12 0HD

Exmoor Pony Society Glen Farm, Waddicombe, Dulverton, Somerset TA22 9RY

Dartmoor Pony Society Fordons, 17 Clare Court, New Biggin Street, Thaxted, Essex

Shetland Pony Stud-Book Society Pedigree House, 6 Kings Place, Perth PH2 8AD

British Show Jumping Association British Equestrian Centre, Stoneleigh, Kenilworth, Warwicks CV8 2LR.

British Show Hack, Cob and Riding Horse Association Rookwood, Packington Park, Meriden, Warwicks CV7 7HF

Endurance Horse and Pony Society of GB 15 Newport Drive, Alcester, Warwickshire

Western Horseman's Association of GB 36 Old Ford View, Barnet, Herts

British Driving Society 27 Dugard Place, Barford, nr Warwick CV35 8DX

Side Saddle Association Highbury House, Welford, Northants NW6 7HT

British Field Sports Society 59 Kennington Road, London SE1 7PZ

USA

American Horse Council 1700 K Street NW, Washington, DC 20006

American Horse Shows Association 220 East 42nd Street, New York, NY 10017

United States Combined Training Association 1 Winthrop Square, Boston, Massachusetts 02110

American Association of Sheriff Posses and Riding Clubs 8133-B White Settlement Road, Fort Worth, Texas 76108

United States Pony Clubs 303 High Street, West Chester, Pennsylvania 19380

American Quarter Horse Association Box 200, Amarillo, Texas 79105

Appaloosa Horse Club Box 8403, Moscow, Idaho 83843

International Arabian Horse Association Box 4502, Burbank, California 91503

Arabian Horse Club Registry of America 332 S. Michigan Avenue, Chicago, Illinois 60604

Standardbred Owners Association 539 Old Country Road, Westbury, NY 11590

Tennessee Walking Horse Breeders and Exhibitors Association 250 N. Ellington Parkway, Lewisburg, Tennessee 37901

American Saddle Horse Breeders Association Inc 929 S. 4th Street, Louisville, Kentucky 40203

American Morgan Horse Association Box 265, Hamilton, NY 13346

American Endurance Ride Conference Inc Box 1605, Auburn, California 95603

North American Trail Ride Conference 1995 Day Road, Gilroy, California 95020

Western States Trail Ride Inc Box 1228, Auburn, California 95603

Glossary

anthelmintic medical preparation for treatment of intestinal worms.

backing stage of breaking and training when by gradual stages the handler eventually sits on the horse's back.

barren mare one who is incapable of conceiving and producing a foal.

bone the measurement of the circumference of bone taken immediately below the knee. A hunter with good bone will measure 21–24 cm ($8\frac{1}{2}$ to $9\frac{1}{2}$ in).

bowed tendons fairly severe leg sprain in which the leg tendons go into a bow shape instead of straight and parallel to the cannon bone; the damage may be permanent.

boxy feet feet with a small frog and a high heel.

brushing the striking of the horse with his leg of the opposite inside fetlock joint of fore or hind leg when moving; injury can be prevented by fitting brushing boots.

cadence the rhythm and tempo of the horse's paces, the horse covering equal distances on the ground in equal spaces of time.

caul (also known as the 'sac') the inner membrane enclosing a foal before birth.

colostrum substance in the mare's milk produced in the first few days after a foal's birth, containing protective constituents.

covert (pronounced 'cover') a hunting term denoting a wood or thicket which might hold a fox or other quarry.

covering the mating of a mare with a stallion.

curbs the thickening of a tendon or ligament just below the point of the hock; may cause lameness.

foal a young horse less than twelve months of age.

foaling slip (also known as a 'Dutch slip') a foal headcollar made of lightweight leather or tubular webbing, adjustable to fit around nose, throat and head, and with a leading tag at the back.

good doer a horse which thrives and keeps in good condition even when not fed the best; opposite of 'bad doer' or 'poor doer'.

grow on to grow and develop.

in-hand describes a horse led with a bridle or headcollar; in a show class indicates unsaddled or without harness, as opposed to a ridden or harness class.

in hand describes a horse which flexes its jaw to the pressure of the reins.

indirect rein (also known as 'neck-reining') the rein when used to press against the horse's neck on the opposite side to which the rider wants him to move, an opposite or bearing rein.

lactating mare a mare producing milk.

lash of lungewhip whipcord attachment at end.

maiden mare one which has never been put to a stallion; *and* a mare which has not had a foal but may be in-foal.

outcross the offspring of two unrelated, or distantly related, horses.

running out used of a stallion turned out to grass with mares who are to mate with him.

scouring (also known as 'purgeing') diarrhoea caused to a foal when feeding from a mare while she is on heat.

shank of a bit the part of the cheekpiece extending below the mouthpiece; on a bit with a curb chain the pressure which can be exerted through leverage on the horse's lower jaw is proportionally stronger according to the length of the shank.

stock of lungewhip the end held in the hand.

straight action describes the movement of a horse whose forelegs move straight and true from the shoulder, the feet remaining in line and the hind legs following the line.

substance possessed by a horse which is well-made, has a good bone and is able to carry a considerable weight for its height.

three-year-old a young horse between its third and fourth birthday; for a racehorse, between 1 January and 31 December of its third year.

tractable easily managed, docile, trainable.

turn away to put a horse out to grass for a period of time as a holiday to rest and unwind.

two-year-old a young horse between its second and third birthday; for a racehorse, between 1 January and 31 December of its second year.

yearling a young horse between its first and second birthday; for a racehorse, between 1 January and 31 December of its first year.

Equivalents of terms in common use

Britain	USA	Britain	USA
back at the knee	calf kneed	numnah	saddle pad
bandages	leg wraps	offset cannons	bench knees
barking foal	barker	on a sixpence	on a dime
broken wind	heaves	over at the knee	calf kneed
brushing	interfering	overreach boots	bell boots
caul	sac	paddock	corral
cracked heel	scratches; greased heel	pervious urachus	persistent urachus
cubes	pellets	plaits	braids
field	paddock	rasp teeth or hooves	float teeth or hooves
fortnight	two weeks	rein back	back
girth	cinch; girth	remove shoes	reset shoes
good doer	good keeper	rise to the trot	post
hacking; riding out	pleasure riding, trail riding	rosette	ribbons
		rug, rugging	blanket, blanketing
halt (long distance rides)	check point	sack	feed bag
		setfast	tying up; azoturia; Monday morning disease
halter	rope halter		
headcollar	halter	show schedules	prize lists
horse box	van	sleepy foal	sleeper
laminitis	founder	society; organization	conference
loose box	box stall	stable rubber	stable towel
lorry	truck	stirrup treads	stirrup pads
lucerne	alfalfa	tarred road	black top
maize	corn	travel a horse	truck a horse
nettlerash	hives	wind galls	wind puffs

Index